"This book is an excellent resource for students interested in an academic career in criminology or criminal justice. Professor Ross provides information relevant to those from a wide variety of life experiences, and helps students solidify their criminology-related career goals and aspirations."

Nathan W. Pino, *Professor, Texas State University*

"*Letters to a Young Criminologist* is a timely and engaging guide for those considering or beginning a career in criminology. Drawing on more than three decades of experience, the author offers candid advice on academic life, educational pathways, career prospects, and the day-to-day realities of teaching and research. Structured as a series of accessible letters, the book challenges misconceptions, highlights opportunities for impact, and bridges the gap between academic criminology and criminal justice practice. Both practical and inspiring, it equips readers with the tools to navigate their careers while underscoring the field's potential to shape policy, scholarship, and justice reform."

Emily I. Troshynski, *Professor of Sociology, University of Nevada*

"*Letters to a Young Criminologist* offers a thoughtful and practical guide for early-career scholars navigating the often uncertain terrain of academia. Drawing from personal reflection, academic research, and real-world experience, Ross provides insights into ways that young criminologists can find their voice and values as scholars. With a reflective and accessible tone, this collection of letters serves as a much-needed form of mentorship in a profession where such guidance is often lacking."

Heith Copes, *Distinguished Professor of Criminal Justice, University of Alabama at Birmingham*

LETTERS TO A YOUNG CRIMINOLOGIST

Building on nearly three dozen books using a similar format, *Letters to a Young Criminologist* provides a long-overdue, valuable, and engaging analysis and advice for individuals considering a career as an academic criminologist.

Drawing on the author's three decades of experience as a criminologist working in government and university settings, academic research, personal experience, and numerous conversations with students, administrators, and fellow criminologists over the years, the book offers helpful, practical, and highly accessible insights for experts and nonspecialists alike. Key features include:

- Offers helpful, practical, and valuable analysis and advice for people considering a career as an academic criminologist.
- Is tailored primarily to undergraduate and graduate students and untenured assistant professors, but is also relevant to a broader audience.
- Draws on the author's extensive experience and scholarly research and combines research and personal anecdotes.
- Provides accessible insights for both specialists and those new to the field.

While the book is primarily directed at undergraduate and graduate students and early-career academics in this increasingly popular academic field/discipline, its insights are equally relevant to criminal justice practitioners and professionals, including people contemplating or currently working in law enforcement, corrections, probation, or parole as officers, court personnel, and criminal lawyers.

Jeffrey Ian Ross, PhD, is Professor in the School of Criminal Justice, College of Public Affairs, and Research Fellow in the Center for International and Comparative Law and the Schaefer Center for Public Policy at the University of Baltimore.

LETTERS TO A YOUNG CRIMINOLOGIST

Jeffrey Ian Ross

LONDON AND NEW YORK

Designed cover image: Illustration from Tasakorn Kongmoon/Alamy Stock Photo

First published 2026
by Routledge
4 Park Square, Milton Park, Abingdon, Oxon OX14 4RN

and by Routledge
605 Third Avenue, New York, NY 10158

Routledge is an imprint of the Taylor & Francis Group, an informa business

British Library Cataloguing-in-Publication Data
A catalogue record for this book is available from the British Library

ISBN: 9781032812991 (hbk)
ISBN: 9781032812984 (pbk)
ISBN: 9781003499145 (ebk)

DOI: 10.4324/9781003499145

Typeset in Sabon
by Deanta Global Publishing Services, Chennai, India

To the students and early-career criminologists whose questions inspired this book.

CONTENTS

ABOUT THE AUTHOR

Jeffrey Ian Ross, PhD, is Professor in the School of Criminal Justice, College of Public Affairs, and Research Fellow in the Center for International and Comparative Law and the Schaefer Center for Public Policy at the University of Baltimore. He has been Visiting Professor at Ruhr University in Bochum, Germany, and the University of Padua, Italy.

Ross has researched, written, and lectured primarily on corrections, policing, political crime, state crime, crimes of the powerful, violence, street culture, graffiti and street art, and crime and justice in American Indian communities for over three decades. His work has appeared in many academic journals and books, as well as popular media. He is the author, coauthor, editor, or coeditor of several books, including most recently *Introduction to Convict Criminology* (2024).

Ross is a respected subject matter expert for local, regional, national, and international news media. He has made live appearances on CNN, CNBC, Fox News Network, MSNBC, and NBC. Additionally, Ross has written op-eds for *The (Baltimore) Sun*, the *Baltimore Examiner*, *The (Maryland) Daily Record*, *The Gazette*, *The Hill*, *Inside Higher Ed*, and *The Tampa Tribune*.

From 1995 to 1998, Ross was Social Science Analyst with the National Institute of Justice, a division of the U.S. Department of Justice. In 2003, he was awarded the University of Baltimore's Distinguished Chair in Research Award. Ross is the co-founder of Convict Criminology and the former co-chair/chair of the Division on Critical Criminology and Social Justice (2014–2017) of the American Society of Criminology. In 2018, Ross was given the Hans W. Mattick Award, "for an individual who has made a distinguished contribution to the field of Criminology & Criminal Justice practice," from the University of Illinois at Chicago. In 2020, he received the John Howard Award from the Academy of Criminal Justice Sciences' Division of Corrections. The award is the ACJS Corrections Section's most prestigious award and was given because of his "outstanding research and service to the field of corrections." In 2020, he was honored with the John Keith Irwin Distinguished Professor Award from the ASC Division of Convict Criminology.

ACKNOWLEDGMENTS

Many people helped with this project, and I am grateful for their assistance. To begin with, thanks to Tom Sutton, Commissioning Editor, and Vanshika Chaudhary, Editorial Assistant, who managed the submission and coordinated the publication process.

Kudos to Rachel Reynolds for initially editing selected portions of this book.

I am indebted to Dakotu Ross-Cabrera for preparing the initial cover deign.

Anonymous reviewers of the book proposal and draft also assisted me in improving the focus of this work.

That being said, over the years, several individuals, including some who have passed away, have shaped my thinking about crime, criminals, the criminal justice system, and what it means to be a criminologist. They include but are not limited to: Andy Aresti, Gregg Barak, Barbara Barraza Uribe, James Binnall, Jessica Bird, Stefano Bloch, Suzanne Brumby, K.C. Carceral, Lukas Carey, Heith Copes, Francis (Frank) T. Cullen, Sacha Darke, Thomas Feltes, Seth Ferranti, Jeff Ferrell, Larry French, David O. Friedrichs, Ted Robert Gurr, Mark S. Hamm, Keith Hayward, Irving Louis Horowitz, Stephen Hughes, Michael Irwin, Rick Jones, Victor Kappeler, Elton Kalica, Daniel Kavish, Ronald L. Kramer (University of Western Michigan), Ron Kramer (Auckland University), Sebastian Kurtenbach, John F. Lennon, Mike Lenza, Peter Manning, Shadd Maruna, Gary T. Marx, Ray Michalowski, Stephen Muzzatti, Greg Newbold, Susan A. Phillips, Nathan Pino, Stephen C. Richards, Dawn L. Rothe, Michael Rowe, Vincenzo Ruggiero, Marty Schwartz, Tobias Singelnstein, Richard Tewksbury, Grant Tietjen,

Austin T. Turk, Francesca Vianello, Loïc Wacquant, Robert Weide, Frank (Trey) Williams, Aaron Z. Winter, Barbara Zaitzow, and Miguel Zaldivar.

From my childhood to my multiple work experiences, I also recognize the debt I owe to numerous friends, co-workers, colleagues, bosses, instructors, contributors to my edited and co-edited books, students, acquaintances, and strangers too numerous to list.

Thanks to the countless people who have been affected by the criminal justice system, not just the victims, but criminal justice professionals, people whose job it's to respond to crime, criminals, criminality, and victims of crimes, for sharing with me their stories and insights, but more importantly their humanity as they perform some of the most challenging jobs in the world. Hats off to the incarcerated and formerly incarcerated individuals, volunteers, paraprofessionals, and activists who shared with me their perspectives on crime, criminal justice, the legal system, especially the field of corrections, and their experiences with incarceration and reentry. Kudos to the numerous individuals, including students (at the undergraduate and graduate levels) and colleagues, who have reached out to me over the years, asking for advice about being an empathic and effective criminologist. Several of their questions have formed the basis of this book.

As always, I want to acknowledge the significant role played by Natasha J. Cabrera, PhD, my wife; Dakota Ross-Cabrera, PhD, and Keanu Ross-Cabrera, MA, our children, who accompanied me on this long, engaging, and mostly enjoyable journey.

INTRODUCTION

Why this book matters

Letters or questions in the field/discipline of criminology

News media stories, commercial movies, popular television shows, social media posts, and documentaries about crime, criminals, victims, and criminal justice capture the public's attention.[1]

This awareness, along with the promise of a steady paycheck, comparatively good working conditions, salary and benefits, and the possibility of helping others, leads some individuals to become criminal justice practitioners and professionals (terms I use interchangeably throughout this book).

Some of these people even consider becoming criminologists.

But not all individuals who have the job title of criminologist do the same type of work.[2] The label criminologist is used in two basic occupational settings. The first refers to people who work within a public safety or criminal justice agency (most commonly, a law enforcement organization). These people are mainly responsible for gathering, assembling, and analyzing crime data and presenting their findings to a broader audience. The second are the individuals who typically work in university settings (usually in a department, school, or college of criminology or criminal justice), have earned a PhD in the discipline of criminology/criminal justice or a cognate/allied discipline (e.g., political science, sociology, etc.), and publish scholarly work relevant to the field of criminology/criminal justice.[3] This book addresses the questions and choices faced by undergraduate and graduate students contemplating becoming academic criminologists (hereafter criminologists), untenured criminologists, and others aspiring to hold this type of position.

The book is also most relevant to people working in criminology/criminal justice who live in the United States and, to a lesser degree, other

DOI: 10.4324/9781003499145-1

Anglo-American democracies like Canada, the United Kingdom, Australia, and New Zealand.

Nevertheless, few people grow up dreaming of being a criminologist. More often, instructors and professors, at least those I know, fall into the profession and remain in it because it offers better alternatives than other available jobs. This isn't to deny that critical and often unrecognized forces may push someone to become a criminologist. For example, about a third of my childhood friends became criminals or were justice-impacted, another third got jobs in law enforcement, and the balance became lawyers. And that's why I often say, drawing on Robert Frost's poem, "The Road Not Taken" (1916) and Scott M. Peck's book, *The Road Less Traveled* (1978), that I took the path few in my neighborhood chose.

Nevertheless, in a somewhat complementary manner, over the past few decades, the idea that criminology is a rendezvous field or discipline has gained traction among some criminologists (and outside observers). In principle, the expression implies that criminology/criminal justice is a multidisciplinary subject, and, over time, a scholar's research is either more or less within the realm of criminology/criminal justice. This is demonstrated in some respects by the name of the academic department they work in or for and the subject matter/content of their publications.

With that in mind, there are many competing academic, popular, cultural, and societal messages about what the field of criminology/criminal justice is and what criminologists do. Why? There is an abundance of information (some of questionable quality) available via the web, articles published in popular media (i.e., newspapers, magazines, and blogs), books that fit in the true crime genre, and publications about Criminology (the study of the causes and effects of crime) and its sister discipline Criminal Justice (the analysis of the dynamics of police, corrections, courts, and juvenile justice). Some of this content is pitched to academics, while others are produced for practitioners, students, and the general public. However, what has yet to be published is a relatively accessible and comprehensive book that explains what an academic criminologist does, how to become a criminologist, and how to survive and perhaps find success in that profession.

Resources for people who are considering a career as an academic criminologist

The academic discipline of criminology/criminal justice can trace its roots back to the late 1880s when Gabriele Tarde conducted statistical analyses of homicide rates in France. Slowly, selected academics and practitioners in Europe (notably Italy and England) and the United States started contributing to a diverse scholarly discipline that examined crime, criminals, and branches of the criminal justice system.

Although the International Association of Chiefs of Police (IACP) was established in 1893, and the American Institute of Criminal Law and Criminology was founded in 1909, the American Society of Criminology (ASC) was not created until 1941. This organization promoted a broader approach to the empirical study of crime and criminal justice. It was designed to serve as a platform for people (nominally criminologists) conducting research in the field.

In 1950, not long after the creation of the ASC, the first School/Department of Criminology was established (by August Vollmer) at the University of California, Berkeley. Since then, the discipline has become ensconced inside the hallowed halls of academia, supported (at least in the United States) by the American Society of Criminology (ASC) and the Academy of Criminal Justice Sciences (ACJS) (formed in 1963), each serving a slightly different constituency.[4]

Predictably, numerous scholarly and textbook publications that address issues in criminology and criminal justice have been published, as have academic journals devoted to different aspects of the discipline. Since the mid-1990s, criminology/criminal justice has become one of the most popular majors in many community colleges and universities in the United States and several other Western countries.

Unquestionably, many instructors use traditional introductory texts for pedagogical purposes. These often weighty and costly tomes are designed to review a broad number of subcomponents of a larger topic that teaching personnel (not to mention reviewers and publishers) believe are important and in which students might be interested. These works are relatively helpful reference tools for the field, and their ideas are typically the basis of significant discussions held by people interested in and/or working in the criminology/criminal justice field. Thus, they are necessary to the discipline's pedagogy.

That said, many other academic books explain and analyze selective aspects of criminology and criminal justice. These are essential building blocks that help readers understand this subject matter. Although a handful of texts provide advice on what students can do with an undergraduate degree in criminology or criminal justice, *few explain to current, prospective, actual, or junior assistant professors what becoming an academic criminologist entails.*

This creates a formidable challenge. A complementary and engaging career-relevant book could serve as a valuable resource alongside the current texts, especially for the previously mentioned audience.

The letters to a young reader model

Almost a century ago, Austrian poet Rainer Maria Rilke wrote a well-respected and cited book, *Letters to a Young Poet* (1929). This book became a mainstay, not simply in the field of poetry, but also in broader literature courses. *Letters to a Young Poet* attempts to dispel the sentimental, glamorous myths of being a poet and replaces them with a sober, almost ascetic vision of artistic life, one grounded in self-examination, solitude, and deep personal necessity.

Seventy-two years after the publication of the original German volume, U.S. publisher Basic Books used Rilke's classic monograph as a model to produce fifteen books in their Art of Mentoring series. This effort began with Alan Dershowitz's *Letters to a Young Lawyer* (2001) and stopped with Jonathan Sama's *Letters to a Young Jew* (2008). It also included works by well-respected individuals including Todd Gitlin, Christopher Hitchens, and O. W. Wilson.

Since then, about three dozen books using the "Letters to a Young" theme (which can also be considered a model or a genre) have been published, including, most recently, Chris Bosh's *Letters to a Young Athlete* (2021). These efforts tend to be composed in one of two ways: The books are written by someone toward the end of their career, either as an act of reflection on their professional engagement or as a guide to people considering a particular profession or subject.

Although the "Letters to a Young... " model can be helpful, many of these books have significant drawbacks. These include, but are not limited to, the fact that:

- they can unnecessarily simplify complex topics,
- the prose style can be meandering and pretentious,
- they reflect the personal bias of the author,
- they may fail to consider alternative perspectives,
- some of the advice is dated (this is especially problematic in rapidly changing fields),
- sometimes, the tone is elitist (the writers start from a privileged position, making the advice less relevant to those from diverse backgrounds or socioeconomic circumstances),
- some of the books emphasize philosophical musings, life wisdom, and long-term vision and can sometimes lack practical, actionable steps, and
- some are idealistic visions of artistry, careers, or ethics, which can be inspiring but do not adequately address the real-world challenges that people entering the profession experience.

Nevertheless, perhaps a book using similar elements of the "Letters to a Young" genre but being mindful of its limitations could assist people considering becoming academic criminologists or those in their early years of the profession. Thus, it's time for a book like *Letters to a Young Criminologist.*

Why else is a book like *Letters to a Young Criminologist* not simply valuable but necessary?

There are several additional reasons why a book like *Letters to a Young Criminologist* is not only valuable but necessary.

First, since the mid-1990s, the number of students, particularly graduate ones, studying criminology/criminal justice at colleges and universities in advanced industrialized countries has increased. This has been driven by a general rise in crime, increased media attention, public fascination with cops and criminals, and a desire among some people at the beginning of their careers to become Criminal Justice professionals.

Second, some practitioner-oriented textbooks that fall under the theme "how to become a Criminal Justice professional" have been published (e.g., Burns, 2023; Johnson, 2018; Pittaro, 2021; Sheridan & Lalka, 2022), but none explore becoming an academic criminologist.

Third, a handful of memoirs either in chapter (e.g., Geiss & Dodge, 2014; Hayward et al., 2009; Powell, 2009) or book form (e.g., Radzinowicz, 2002; Pepinsky, 2006; Yablonsky, 2010; Barak, 2020) written by criminologists, have been released. Although a few of these efforts provide advice on the profession, the information isn't organized in an easily digestible manner.

Fourth, as of this writing, only one book has been published that reviews the complex and nuanced issues connected to being an academic criminologist in a relatively comprehensive and understandable manner. *How to Find Success as a Criminal Justice Faculty Member* (2017), edited by Craig Hemmens, consists of eight chapters covering fundamental issues connected to becoming a criminologist, advancing in the field, professional development, and through different ranks. These chapters, originally appeared in a special issue of the *Journal of Criminal Justice Education* in 2016. Although some of the advice is timely, other pieces are outdated or generic because they do not necessarily apply to criminology and criminal justice but are generalizable to almost all social science disciplines.

Fifth, some of the advice given to criminology/criminal justice undergraduate and graduate students and criminologists at the early stages of their career that is published in the discipline-relevant scholarly journals and newsletters produced by the learned societies in our profession is often:

- generic in tone,
- not necessarily specific to the fields of criminology/criminal justice (it can apply to graduate students and junior colleagues in almost any social science discipline),
- unrealistic in practice,
- only applicable to ideal situations, or
- only helpful in best-case scenarios.

Undoubtedly, undergraduate and graduate students, academics, regardless of their employment status, and members of the general public can go to the web (or even ChatGPT, Claude AI, or another similar artificial intelligence website) and find out how to become an academic criminologist. Still, the information that they retrieve is of varying and questionable quality, limited specificity, and these sources may not answer all or even most of the questions users may have. Likewise, the newsletters and some journals (e.g., *Journal of Criminal Justice Education*) of the American Society of Criminology and Academy of Criminal Justice Sciences (as well as those run by the British Society of Criminology and the Australian and New Zealand Society of Criminology), the most prominent learned organizations for the scholarly study of crime and criminal justice, frequently publish articles aimed at assisting both aspiring and journeymen criminologists. These types of articles, however, appear on a sporadic basis. That is why a book that is focused on examining the intricacies of the profession, written by a criminologist like me, someone who is respected and familiar with the multifaceted complexities of the field of criminology/criminal justice, including the long-standing and current debates in the discipline, can be helpful. And from a publisher's point of view, this book can be revised every few years and updated by integrating new research and developments in the discipline.

Thus, a comprehensive, up-to-date, and engaging book on career choice and expectations related to the field of contemporary criminology/criminal justice that integrates scholarly research, personal experience, and interviews to explain profession-relevant issues, the people who engage in this activity, and reactions to it, which is also accessible to nonspecialists interested in the subject matter is needed. To the extent necessary, *Letters to a Young Criminologist* also reviews causes, reactions, and potential solutions to challenges that many professors of criminology/criminal justice face.

How will I prevent the major pitfalls with this genre?

This monograph considers the long-standing and changing nature of the academic discipline of criminology/criminal justice, Criminal justice agencies, and university education in this field. Unlike some pieces written by academic criminologists, it treats the subject matter comprehensively and strives to be engaging.

Thus, *Letters to a Young Criminologist* builds not only on my scholarly research and practitioner experience, but also on my weekly blog that deals, in part, with issues that criminologists face during their careers, and issues that undergraduate and graduate students who are entering the discipline may experience. In addition to being of interest and accessible to the previously mentioned audience, *Letters to a Young Criminologist* is relevant to criminal justice professionals, other social scientists, members of the news media, lawyers thinking of changing careers, and other nonspecialists.

That being said, the reader of this book should be cautioned that the advice dispensed in *Letters to a Young Criminologist* may also be a product of the era during which it was written, my unique circumstances, and those of my colleagues I've interacted with over the years. In other words, although what I've written made sense to me and many of my fellow criminologists coming up in the profession, the information imparted may seem foreign or outdated in a decade or so. Why? Numerous changes and challenges are currently facing the academy, especially in the United States, and this will inevitably trickle down to the subject specializations.

This includes, but isn't limited to, developments in numerous states that are curtailing (or attempting to ban) the teaching of subjects such as Critical Race Theory and placing restrictions on curricula related to Diversity, Equity, and Inclusion (DEI). Also, advances in instructional technology, spurred by the COVID-19 pandemic (2020–2022), such as Zoom, the introduction of artificial intelligence, like ChatGPT, and the increasing reliance on online teaching, have impacted the academic discipline of criminology/criminal justice.

While I doubt universities will cease to exist anytime soon, how they pursue their mission will likely change regarding the constituencies they serve, how they operate, and whom they hire to help achieve their goals (Ross, 2022). These changes may affect their reward, promotion, and organizational structures and the norms shaping academic life in the near future.

Challenges I faced while writing this book

Writing a book of this nature presented several challenges. These can be divided into eight overlapping areas. I discuss them here from least to most important.

Process of Knowledge Production

To begin with, there were many ways to proceed with this project. One method I've used in the past (Ross, 2001; Ross & Shanty, 2009) would have been to contact academic criminologists and other experts in criminology/criminal justice and ask them to write a chapter in their area of specialization. This process is often facilitated by holding a series of panels at American Society of Criminology (ASC) or the Academy of Criminal Justice Sciences (ACJS) conferences as a vehicle to gather individual contributions. However, this method isn't as easy as it sounds. It's labor-intensive, and there is no guarantee that I would receive a full complement of valuable submissions. Moreover, none of the English language "Letters to a Young" books in print are edited collections. Thus, my approach would significantly depart from the previously outlined genre.

Another potential method was the one utilized by American entrepreneur, author, and podcaster Tim Ferriss. I could have started a podcast and invited criminologists to discuss the lessons they had learned over the years, distilling this wisdom into a coherent whole. Again, this would have been a long, resource-intensive, and tedious process.

I also considered contacting the American Society of Criminology and the Academy of Criminal Justice Sciences to propose conducting a major survey of their memberships. Although this would be a significant undertaking, I was doubtful about the response rate and, by extension, the data quality I would get. Like the previous two strategies, this approach would also be very costly.

Similar to the previously mentioned alternatives, none of the published books following the "Letters to a Young" model surveyed their membership. For example, Christopher Hitchens, author of *Letters to a Young Contrarian*, did not interview or survey a single journalist like him.

Editorial control and narrative structure

Ultimately, this book takes a singular position on the profession. However, it's informed by my experience, the individuals I've interacted with over the years, and the scholarship I've read on this subject.[5] I exerted as much editorial control as possible over the project, allowing me to shape a coherent narrative that closely aligns with my vision for this book.

Genre and disciplinary considerations

Books with the expression "Letters to a Young" in their title are part of a genre that exhibits diversity in approach. Some works take a memoir-like method, whereas others focus on sage-like dispensation of advice. Others books blend both approaches and try to provide balance. This latter style is the one I've taken in *Letters to a Young Criminologist*.

Defining and delimiting the scope

A major challenge was ensuring that the questions asked and answered in each chapter/letter were most relevant to criminology/criminal justice, not just any social science.

Numerous helpful books offer graduate students and early career professors in the social sciences advice on the challenges of being an academic (including moving up the ranks, publishing, etc.).[6] But that's not what I want to achieve here. Thus, if I determined that a topic was not unique to criminologists (e.g., Should criminologists collaborate with other criminologists to coauthor articles and other scholarly works? What grants are available to graduate students?), then, in general, I decided not to address this issue.

Although I recognize that there are many types of criminologists, this book is directed toward people who want to work in a university setting as an instructor or professor of Criminology/Criminal Justice rather than in a relevant government agency or for a research consulting firm.

Success and happiness in academia

An underlying issue that this book addresses, particularly in the conclusion, is the relationship between success and happiness in one's career, job, profession, and work, terms that do not mean the same thing. Although there is a strong connection among these concepts or states of being in any career, being successful as an academic criminologist does not necessarily equate to being happy. Many external factors must be considered when we focus on this situation.

Balancing empirical and subjective experience

Where possible, I support my claims with empirical evidence from scholarly literature that directly addresses the core questions of each chapter. However, in many cases, these questions have not been rigorously explored within Criminology, Criminal Justice, or related disciplines. In those cases, the letters reflect my interpretations and analytic judgements informed by existing research and professional experience. This approach may challenge the assumptions of some academics who view Criminology, Criminal Justice, and the social sciences as purely objective or value-neutral (or believe it should be). I don't share this view. Some arguments in this book involve inference and speculation, informed by my personal experiences and those of my colleagues.

Challenges in academic writing and publishing

Another hurdle included separating content that speaks to being an academic and/or university professor from that which resonates most with being a criminology/criminal justice professor.[7] There are things that might help you get your first academic job in criminology/criminal justice, but not only have others done a good job writing about this (e.g., Alarid, 2016), but many of these articles are typically not specific to the field of criminology.

Variability in content and organization

Not all letters are the same length. Although some readers may have difficulties with this approach, there is no logical reason why each letter should be as long as the last one. Some issues demand more thoughtful responses, whereas others do not require as much elaboration. More specifically, I may have more to say about one issue than another. Also, some letters are more interesting or relevant to individual readers. Thus, it's perfectly fine if readers choose to skip one or more letters.

Finally, another important concern involved how to optimally organize the letters/questions. I considered two basic paths. On the one hand, the letters could be arranged from least to most necessary based on what I think most readers of *Letters to a Young Criminologist* would be interested in. On the other hand, I decided to arrange the letters/questions around five basic themes:

- Perception and image of the academic field of criminology/criminal justice
- Educational path/s and training
- Job prospects and career trajectories
- Instruction/teaching
- Research and service
- Reflections

Prominent themes that *Letters to a Young Criminologist* deals with

Letters to a Young Criminologist is divided into 51 letters, each dealing with a different issue or question facing someone considering or currently working in the academic field of criminology/criminal justice.

Some of these questions have been previously explored by scholars who have gathered evidence, analyzed it, and published their research in academic venues. However, the scope and rigor of some of this research have varied, with some studies being more methodologically sound than others. Additionally, many of these findings may now be outdated due to changes in context or newer data. Beyond academic sources, relevant popular works also attempt to answer some of these questions. Although these platforms may not always meet scholarly standards, they often provide valuable insights for a broader audience.

Each letter attempts to integrate the existing literature, drawing on a wide range of sources to systematically present the most comprehensive and high-quality research, addressing every question and highlighting the remaining gaps and weaknesses. It will also try to leave the reader with a critical lesson. Some of the questions are interrelated and may be linked together.

Letters to a Young Criminologist explores not only the hurdles that prospective and actual graduate students (and recently minted doctoral students) in criminology and criminal justice face, but also provides answers to questions they may have about pursuing graduate studies, their perceptions of the quality of their education, and their career aspirations.

The book also examines challenges that recent criminology and criminal justice graduates face in the academic job market, including the importance of networking. It also explores the difficulty that academic criminologists may face in achieving work-life balance and offers strategies for managing competing demands.

Letters to a Young Criminologist draws on my experiences and those of criminology and criminal justice doctoral graduates and early-career academic criminologists. It conveys empirically based trends, including perceptions of graduate training and insights into job and career satisfaction, as shared by colleagues and peers.

Why did I write this book?

There are several reasons why I wrote this book, and I've ranked them in order from least to most important.

One of the important responsibilities professors have is to mentor those coming up in the field and to extend a helping hand to "colleagues" that we believe are deserving of assistance, who have difficulty understanding the nuances of the profession. This approach has been central to the Convict Criminology praxis, with which I've been involved since its founding. At this stage in my career, I feel well positioned to offer constructive guidance to junior scholars; advice grounded in my professional experience, not just speculation.

Over the years, I've interacted with a wide range of criminologists and other social scientists, and I've also encountered more than my fair share of bad career advice, some of it from well-meaning colleagues, friends, instructors, mentors, or relatives. If I had uncritically followed all of it, I might have ended up alienating many people in my profession, torpedoing my career, and eventually abandoning the academy altogether. In this book, I try to share the insights I wish I'd learned earlier, helping readers see what truly matters and what can be ignored.

True confessions

In the spirit of full disclosure, when contemplating graduate school and seeking the advice of my undergraduate mentors at the time (including noted criminologist Austin T. Turk), I applied not only to criminology/criminal justice graduate programs but to political science ones as well. Although I was accepted to master's programs at highly ranked universities in both fields, I decided to study under Ted Robert Gurr, a well-respected scholar of conflict processes, who was working in a department of Political Science. During my doctoral studies, I took my first and only graduate-level course in criminal justice, which consisted of having a few conversations over a summer semester with a professor and earning a grade. In the end, although I earned my PhD in political science, I only worked in that discipline for three years during the early part of my career. Why, then, did I shift to criminology/criminal justice? Two reasons stand out. First, when I applied to tenure-track jobs, the Criminology/Criminal Justice departments were more interested in my scholarly work than Political Science ones. Second, I liked hanging out with criminologists I met more than with the political scientists.

I also recognize that many of my professional colleagues would not consider me to be a mainstream criminologist. While defining a mainstream criminologist is difficult, they generally operate within dominant paradigms, and rely on widely accepted theories, methods, and policy perspectives. Their research tends to be relatively uncontroversial, quantitatively focused, and concentrated in a few subject specializations. They also prioritize publishing in top-tier criminology journals. In contrast, I typically identify with critical criminology, which challenges conventional frameworks and engages with issues that may not fit within the dominant narratives of criminology and criminal justice.

That said, many people, often influenced by television shows and other popular media, have misconceptions about what criminologists do. They usually mistakenly assume that we're forensic experts analyzing blood spatter, DNA, and gunshot residue or that we live dramatic, action-packed lives like those portrayed by characters on TV. In reality, criminology is a field rooted in understanding crime's causes, societal responses, and the impact of criminal justice policies; work that can be both monotonous and tedious, but also interesting and deeply rewarding, though far removed from the Hollywood version.

Additional features of the book

Introduction

Letters to a Young Criminologist integrates not only my experience with academic criminology/criminal justice but also those of my colleagues whom I've observed and who have shared their stories with me. The book also reviews long-standing, current, and relevant scholarship in criminology/criminal justice research and work available in popular media venues. The letters will occasionally reference current events in the criminology/criminal justice world by relying on selected interviews, recent news media accounts, and information from respected news outlets. (Other important matters are discussed below in alphabetical order.)

Audience

Letters to a Young Criminologist will primarily appeal to readers interested in becoming academic criminologists or Criminal Justice professionals. The book would also be helpful to graduate students and the general public who want to know what criminologists do. *Letters to a Young Criminologist* may also interest select practitioners and professionals (i.e., law enforcement, corrections, and probation and parole officers). Members of the news media covering stories that may touch on criminology/criminal justice may also be interested in the book. Instructors who teach the subject of criminology/criminal justice at the undergraduate and graduate levels may assign the book to their students. *Letters to a Young Criminologist* will appeal not only to readers in the United States but also to other Anglophone countries and those nations where English is a dominant second language. Thus, the audience is international in scope.

Courses where this book might be used

In terms of classroom usage, this book would be most appropriate for undergraduate and graduate studies in criminology/criminal justice. It has secondary use in the cognate disciplines of sociology, psychology, public policy, and criminal law.

How to use this book/How should the reader approach this book?

Letters to a Young Criminologist is designed so readers can explore the letters at any point in the book. Nevertheless, I encourage them to go through the letters chronologically or start with one that sparks their interest and then move to the next appealing one. The letters are intended to be bite-sized and easily completed in one sitting. This flexibility also allows instructors using the book in one or more courses to assign specific groups of letters for review; all the letters don't need to be covered by a reader or included in an assignment.

Reading level

The reading level is targeted toward readers with some university education (at least upper-level university students) and graduate students. *Letters to a*

Young Criminologist will be easy to read and designed to answer common questions this audience asks about the subject matter.

Timeliness

Because academia constantly changes, it's important to remember that some of the advice I give may not stand the test of time. In a decade, students and colleagues might find this information interesting but less relevant to their immediate circumstances. By then, universities may have either ceased to exist in their current form or transformed significantly. This evolution will likely extend to fields like criminology and criminal justice, which continue to splinter and diversify as new knowledge develops, learning technology advances, and university budgets fluctuate.

Writing style

The book is written in a conversational tone, as if I were talking with a graduate student I'm mentoring or a junior colleague I'm advising, in a relaxed setting. That is why you will see contractions in sentences, the occasional use of colloquialisms, and minimal citations.

Summing up

In sum, *Letters to a Young Criminologist* is the go-to book for anyone contemplating becoming an academic criminologist. It's informative, integrates current scholarly research and popular debates, and is engaging. Writing it has been a blast, well, most of the time.

Notes

1 Some readers may have difficulty with my use of terms like criminal, prisoner, or inmate, preferring more humanizing alternatives such as incarcerated person, formerly incarcerated, justice-impacted, or justice-involved. Each term has its context, and in certain situations, some may be more appropriate than others. My rationale for these choices is discussed in greater detail elsewhere (e.g., Ross, 2024).

2 Over time, I've found that people often use terms like career, job, calling, profession, etc. interchangeably, sometimes leading to unnecessary confusion. To improve clarity throughout the book, I define and discuss these distinctions in Appendix A.

3 Throughout this book, I emphasize the expression "earning a PhD," rather than getting, obtaining, etc. For my rationale, see, for example, "What's wrong with most synonyms for earning a certification, degree, diploma, or licensure?" https://jeffreyianross.com/whats-wrong-with-most-synonyms-for-earning-a-certification-degree-diploma-or-licensure/ (Downloaded March 7, 2025).

4 Other important learned organizations in the academic fields of criminology/criminal justice include the British Society of Criminology, the Australian and New Zealand Society of Criminology, and the European Society of Criminology. Many other countries have learned societies that serve as the principal scholarly bodies for criminology/criminal justice, but the issues they cover are more national in scope.
5 Over the past three and a half decades, a considerable debate about the definition of scholarship has been sparked by Ernest Boyer's *Scholarship Reconsidered* (1990) and Pat Hutchings, Mary Huber, and Anthony Ciccone, *The Scholarship of Teaching: New Elaborations, New Developments* (1997). Although Boyer's expanded view of scholarship has been influential, I generally prefer a more traditional conception that emphasizes original research and publication as the core of scholarly work.
6 These are listed in Appendix B.
7 In most institutions of higher education (colleges and universities), tenured and tenure-track professors are usually required to do three things: engage in scholarship, teaching, and service.

References and suggested reading

Alarid, L. F. (2016). How to secure your first academic job out of graduate school. *Journal of Criminal Justice Education*, *27*(2), 160–174.

Ballard, J. D., Klein, M. C., & Dean, A. (2007). Mentoring for success in criminal justice and criminology: Teaching professional socialization in graduate programs. *Journal of Criminal Justice Education, 18*(2), 283–297.

Barak, G. (2020). *Chronicles of a radical criminologist: Working the margins of law, power, and justice*. Rutgers University Press.

Burns, R. G. (2023). *Careers in criminal justice and criminology*. Routledge Publishers.

Geiss, G., & Dodge, M. (Eds.). (2014). *Lessons of criminology*. Routledge Publishers.

Hayward, K., Maruna, S., & Mooney, J. (Eds.). (2009). *Fifty key thinkers in criminology*. Routledge Publishers.

Hemmens, C. (2017). *How to find success as a criminal justice faculty member*. Routledge Publishers.

Hoover, K. B., & Lucas, K. T. (2023). Mentoring graduate students: A study on academic rejection, the pressure to publish, and career paths. *Journal of Criminal Justice Education*, *35*(1), 195–217.

Johnson, C. H. (Ed.). (2018). *Careers in criminal justice*. Sage Publications.

Kim, B., Stallings, R. P., Merlo, A. V., & Lin, A. W. C. (2015). Mentoring in criminology and criminal justice doctoral education: Doctoral program coordinators' perspectives. *Journal of Criminal Justice Education*, *26*(4), 390–407.

Kunselman, J., Hensley, C., & Tewksbury, R. (2003). Mentoring in academe: Models for facilitating academic development. *Journal of Criminal Justice Education*, *14*(1), 17–35.

Moak, S. C., & Walker, J. T. (2014). How to be a successful mentor. *Journal of Contemporary Criminal Justice*, *30*(4), 427–442.

Pepinsky, H. E. (2006). *Peacemaking: Reflections of a radical criminologist*. University of Ottawa Press.

Peterson, E. S. L. (1999). Building scholars: A qualitative look at mentoring in a criminology and criminal justice doctoral program. Journal *of Criminal Justice Education*, *10*(2), 247–261.

Pittaro, M. (2021). *Pursuing and navigating a career in criminal justice*. Kendall Hunt.
Powell, D. C. (Ed.). (2009). *Critical voices in criminology*. Lexington Books.
Radzinowicz, L. (2002). *Adventures in criminology*. Routledge Publishers.
Ross, J. I. (2001). How did I get into this mess anyway: Editing books in criminology and criminal justice. *ACJS Today*, *21*(2), 6–9.
Ross, J. I., & Shanty, F. (2009). Editing encyclopedias for fun and aggravation. *Publishing Research Quarterly*, 25(3), 159–169.
Ross, J. I. (2022, May 21). *Most American universities are no longer sustainable in their current form*. Retrieved March 7, 2025, from https://jeffreyianross.com/most-american-universities-are-no-longer-sustainable-in-their-current-form/
Ross, J. I. (2024). *Introduction to convict criminology*. Bristol University Press.
Sheridan, M., & Lalka, T. J. (2022). *Contemporary criminal justice careers*. Rowman & Littlefield.
Yablonsky, L. (2010). *Confessions of a criminologist: Some of my best friends were sociopaths*. iUniverse.

PART I

Perception and image of the academic field of criminology/criminal justice

Letter 1

WHO IS THE REAL CRIMINOLOGIST?[1]

Unless I'm mistaken, there are two situations in which people can legitimately claim to call themselves a criminologist.

In the first instance, many criminal justice agencies and other relevant government organizations hire individuals for the job title "Criminologist." In order to be considered for this position, the applicant must possess the necessary specified qualifications (which typically include but are not limited to a master's degree, usually in the fields of criminology or criminal justice). These individuals collate and analyze crime statistics, or they are involved in the processing of crime scenes.

In the other case, in general, as long as you have earned a PhD in the discipline of criminology/criminal justice from an accredited university and/or you publish a significant amount of your research in peer-reviewed journals or books in the discipline of criminology or criminal justice, you also have a legitimate claim to calling yourself a criminologist.

So what?

Some individuals (often current or retired criminal justice practitioners or people with lived experiences—formerly incarcerated individuals, justice-impacted or involved, etc.) refer to themselves as criminologists.

Lived (sometimes labeled "firsthand") experience can be significant in helping people understand the subtleties of a situation, process, or profession, but in and of itself, lived experience isn't equivalent to certification.

Certification usually requires a person to complete a course of study and training, pass a test, earn a diploma or degree, and/or be granted licensure in a relevant subject area. In principle, this process assists a person in

DOI: 10.4324/9781003499145-3

gaining expertise. On the other hand, while people with lived experience may have valuable insights, criminologists might want to listen to or read what they say or write, and perhaps they have something of interest to add to the discussion; thus, we can learn from them. But again, these individuals may not have recognized, appropriate subject-specific certifications. More precisely, possessing knowledge about crime, criminals, and criminal justice agencies does not grant you credentials, nor does it make you a bona fide criminologist.

Why is calling oneself a criminologist without the appropriate certifications problematic?

To begin with, it's disingenuous to call oneself something when one isn't.

Just because you're a member of the American Society of Criminology, the Academy of Criminal Justice Sciences, or a similar organization does not mean you're a criminologist. And if you stop paying your dues to either of these learned societies, it does not mean you're no longer a criminologist.

Additionally, if almost anyone can call themselves a criminologist without the appropriate or widely agreed-upon criteria, it devalues the expertise of the people who have gone through the long slog of earning the relevant degrees, meeting standards, etc.

Moreover, claiming to be a criminologist without appropriate degrees, publications, etc., while appealing to some people and constituencies, misrepresents what duly credentialed criminologists should know and do.

This isn't an elitist or protectionist interpretation. Earning a doctorate in Criminology, Criminal Justice, or a cognate field from an accredited university and publishing in respected venues means that you have undergone rigorous training and have demonstrated to others with a similar background that you're duly qualified.

This issue adds to widespread confusion about the distinctions and relationships among amateurs, authorities, experts, and professionals. A common source of misunderstanding is the conflation of certification with accreditation. Although the two are related, they are not interchangeable. Clarifying these terms requires careful attention to nuance, ideally supported by dictionary definitions and contextual usage. Without this precision, both individuals and organizations risk making flawed assumptions about authority, competence, expertise, and legitimacy.

Overall, amateurs lack the knowledge, experience, and skills that experts possess. More specifically, experts usually have specialized knowledge and skills and may even have some relevant certification, as may the organizations they work for.

Experts may act unprofessionally (even amateurishly) and have difficulty translating their knowledge to a broader audience. However, as long as they have the appropriate certifications, publications, etc., they are still experts.

Why does this occur?

Unlike the professions of architecture, law, and medicine, the field of criminology/criminal justice does not have a widely recognized method to certify individuals as criminologists. Neither does it have a professional organization to determine and enforce licensing standards or to sanction those who call themselves criminologists but do not have the credentials. Thus, anyone who wants to call themselves a criminologist can do so.

How might this problem be addressed?

I have three imperfect solutions to this thorny and persistent problem.

First, criminologists could spend resources (e.g., time, money, etc.) educating the public about who should be labeled a criminologist. Maybe even our learned organizations, like the American Society of Criminology (ASC) and/or the Academy of Criminal Justice Sciences (ACJS) (and similar organizations in other countries), could do the same.

Second, we might try to convince one or more of our learned organizations to establish a certification or licensing process. The ASC and/or ACJS could experiment with a certification or licensure program for a short period and then evaluate its impact. However, this initiative could become unnecessarily burdensome and exclude people with criminal convictions, similar to what has happened with other large licensure bodies.

Third, criminologists, particularly those who work in university settings, can make it their mission to call out every time they see, meet, or learn of someone who claims erroneously to be a criminologist. Although this may provide personal satisfaction to some in our profession, it also seems to be an exhausting, complicated process, one that my colleagues might equally deem a waste of time.

In reality, I doubt that criminologists care enough about this professional issue and are relatively content to live in a state of ambiguity.

Note

1 An earlier version of this letter was published as "Who is the real criminologist? And other uncomfortable questions about expertise," June 23, 2021. https://jeffreyianross.com/who-is-the-real-criminologist-and-other-uncomfortable-questions-about-expertise/

Suggested reading

Ross, J. I. (2023). *What's wrong with most synonyms for earning a certification, degree, diploma, or licensure?* February 14, 2023. https://jeffreyianross.com/whats-wrong-with-most-synonyms-for-earning-a-certification-degree-diploma-or-licensure/

Wolfgang, M. E. (1963). Criminology and the criminologist. *Journal of Criminal Law, Criminology & Police Science, 54*(1), 155–162.

Letter 2

WHAT ARE THE POSITIVE AND NEGATIVE ASPECTS OF BEING AN ACADEMIC CRIMINOLOGIST?

As previously mentioned, there are a handful of job designations with the title criminologist. However, this book focuses on the people who have earned their doctorates in criminology/criminal justice (or a cognate field) and typically work as university instructional staff, most likely as professors at and for programs, departments, schools, and colleges (hereafter departments) of criminology/criminal justice. These individuals may work in positions formally classified as adjuncts, instructors, part-timers, sessionals, visiting professors, or professors.

With that in mind, some of these jobs (or more specifically, the demands of the work, the environment, compensation, and benefits) are more desirable than others. This varies not only across different educational institutions but also within regions of the same country and internationally. Equally important is the degree of professional autonomy criminologists experience, the respect they receive from colleagues, students, and administrators, the time they have for family and leisure, and the overall quality of life the job affords.

All things being equal, it's necessary to acknowledge that, regardless of the discipline, the quality of work experience is typically better the higher the rank a professor has. This highlights the issue of precarity. Untenured part-timers have less job security, make less money, and have fewer benefits than full-timers. Full and tenured professors are usually better paid, have more benefits, and have more job security.

In order to judge the positive and negative aspects of being an academic criminologist, it's essential to consider numerous factors. These include, but are not limited to, the following interrelated things:

DOI: 10.4324/9781003499145-4

- which college or organizational unit the department is located in;
- the size of the department (how many instructional staff are dedicated to the teaching of criminology/criminal justice, how many students are pursuing their bachelor's degrees, etc.);
- whether the department only has a bachelor's program or also has a master's or even a doctoral program;
- the types of students the department primarily serves;
- the amount of resources the institution devotes to the organizational unit; and
- the teaching, research, and service expectations that the organizational unit places on instructors/professors.

Type of institution of higher education

The type of educational institution where a criminologist works significantly shapes their professional environment, including the students they teach, the colleagues they engage with, and the working conditions they experience. Broadly speaking, academic criminologists tend to be employed at one of two types of institutions (the differences between teaching at a university and a community college is reviewed in another letter in this book.). Further distinctions arise based on whether the institution is publicly funded or privately run.

Since most criminology/criminal justice departments are located in public universities, the likelihood that you will be teaching there is high. Another issue that should be considered is whether the university has a School or College of Law. Inevitably, there may be some interaction between faculty and programs that focus on criminal law and with the department, school, and college of criminology/criminal justice. Deans and provosts may encourage this collaboration. However, this may be wishful thinking. Unfortunately, because of the inherent competition and protectionism traditionally found among organizational units, few financial incentives (e.g., internal grants, lessening of teaching or service obligations) are provided to encourage this kind of partnership. Thus, interdepartmental or intercollege collaboration rarely occurs.

Location of the department in the overall mission of the university

If the department/school is located in a college of public affairs or a liberal arts college, this will also have subtle effects on the types of courses offered, the instructors who work there, and the students who take the classes. The disciplinary location can also affect the respect that department members receive from colleagues in other departments on campus and from the senior administration.

Dissecting your department

In principle, most of your departmental colleagues will be criminologists, hopefully at different career stages. Some instructors, professors, administrators, and staff may be nurturing and supportive; others may be indifferent and show little concern; and a third group may be actively obstructionist and toxic.

If, as it's frequently alleged, some psychologists have mental health issues that draw them to the field (because they're trying to work things out), then it's not too far-fetched to suggest that some criminologists may be psychopaths.

These latter situations can contribute to a department being a source of stress. According to Gabbidion and Higgins (2012),

> Colleagues may cause stress to each other because of disagreements over the direction of the department, jealousy, or other factors. Occasionally, disagreements over minor and more substantive issues can lead to departments that are polarized into different "camps" or cliques... Administrators can also create stress by having unreasonable expectations of faculty, expecting faculty to do more with less, and unfairly distributing resources.(p. 678)

Students

Although a letter that appears later in the book takes a deeper dive into the "typical" criminology/criminal justice student, suffice it to say that undergraduate students who take classes in departments of criminology/criminal justice primarily consist of people who are former, current, or aspiring criminal justice practitioners. Also, some students choose to study or major in criminology/criminal justice because they perceive that the bar is low to earn a bachelor's degree relevant to this professional field. Some assume that criminology/criminal justice will be an easy major because they have watched a lot of true crime shows on television or listened to them as podcasts, find them interesting and enjoyable, and then believe that earning a degree in this subject is a cakewalk. So, when it comes time for them to pursue a degree, they choose criminology/criminal justice. This mix of students has real consequences for how instructors teach and student expectations. As in every academic discipline, some students are genuinely committed to their studies, others are demanding in various ways, whereas others don't appear to have a curious bone in their body.

The primary subject focus of the department

Before continuing, it's necessary to briefly talk about the naming and labeling of academic units. Some organizational units specializing in teaching criminology or criminal justice are called departments, whereas others are called schools or colleges. There is an implicit assumption that as we move from departments to colleges, the organizational unit will be larger (i.e., more instructors, support staff, students, and courses offered and taught). But some of this labeling is simply aspirational, public relations posturing, and/or wishful thinking. In other words, a comparatively small department may call itself a college in the hope of convincing an external audience (mainly prospective students) that they are larger than it actually is. This naming may also be a reflection of a bygone era. At one point in time, the unit was a college. However, due to declining enrollments, strategic initiatives, organizational mismanagement, etc., the number of students the unit attracts has dropped, and the administration has not bothered to change the name to better reflect the current reality.

Although there are standalone departments of criminology and criminal justice, it's not uncommon in the United States and elsewhere for institutions of higher learning to have combined departments, schools, or colleges. These configurations typically include the subject matters of sociology and criminal justice. For students, professors, and departmental chairs, these arrangements can be a blessing or a curse. For example, this situation could enable synergy among instructors, professors, and students in terms of collaboration on research projects and in instructional situations, or competition for scarce resources could potentially arise from this arrangement. Also necessary is that unlike the United States and Canada, many departments or schools of criminology/criminal justice in the United Kingdom and Australia (not to mention Europe and Latin America) are located in schools or colleges of law. This produces its own complex set of challenges.

A related issue is the official naming of the organizational unit in question. Is it called a Department of Criminology or a Department of Criminal Justice, or are both names combined? Is it called the Department of Criminal Justice Sciences or the Department of Social Justice? Ideally, this name should reflect the content of the courses taught and the research interests of professors who work in this unit. Sometimes, it does, and at other times, it does not.

Size of the department

The department's size in terms of faculty members and students will affect workloads and expectations. Some departments have a thousand students, whereas others hobble along with a handful of them. Also, the larger the department, the greater the possibility that it will offer more than bachelor's, master's and doctoral degrees. It also means that in principle, instructors will not be stuck teaching large undergraduate service courses, like "Introduction to Criminology" or "Introduction to Criminal Justice," but can teach the more specific subjects that genuinely interest them at higher levels.

What varies, however, are the expectations that are placed on instructors. This includes how many classes they're required to teach each semester, the types of courses they're expected to teach, the level of instruction (undergraduate versus graduate), the size of those classes, and the extent of the research and service (to the department, college, university, and profession) instructors are expected to do to maintain or advance in their position. This depends on the department, college, and the university they work for. Generally, the work expectations demanded of an academic criminologist at one university are the same among departments at that same educational institution.

Service expectations

In smaller departments, service expectations are often relatively high. This includes serving on and chairing numerous committees. You may also be asked to supervise the criminal justice student association or honors club. Unless this task is centralized at the college or university level, your duties might extend to advising students, which basically means ensuring they are taking the appropriate classes outlined in the student handbook or curriculum manual. In a larger department, this task often falls on the shoulders of one person in the department, or one or more student advisors in the dean's office handle this task.

Teaching responsibilities

In the United States, most criminologists at most four-year universities outside the R1 research core are responsible for teaching what is referred to as a 3/3 load. This means that in the fall semester, they teach three classes, and in the spring, they also teach three. At smaller universities, there are lots of service courses that you will need to teach (e.g., "Introduction to Criminology," "Introduction to Criminal Justice," etc.), and they may not be reflective of your core research specialization. Sometimes, the 3/3 load allows you to teach two sections of the same class, thus relieving some of the preparation burden that teaching six different classes involves.

Research expectations

Some departments have very high research expectations, while others require full-time professors to do very little of this task, if at all. Usually, this is communicated by department chairs and senior professors to junior professors and spelled out in the tenure and promotion documents. However, there are also strong organizational culture elements that are not reflected in these types of communications.

Why do departments, colleges, and universities expect professors to do research? In general, it is reflective of the mission of the department, college, or university. One common belief is that by doing research, you're keeping up to date with development in your field and that this expertise will be translated into the classroom. Also, by engaging in research and maybe even partnering with local criminal justice agencies, you would presumably be well-positioned to provide introductions for your students for internships and potential jobs after graduation. Again, more will be said about research expectations and obligations in letters appearing later in this book.

Organizational expectations of the institution of higher education

In the average university, academic criminologists are typically required to conduct research, teach students, and engage in departmental, college, university, and professional service. The exact percentages of these obligations vary from one professor to another, department, college, and university to another. And what combination of teaching, research, and service might get you tenure and promotion in one context may not be sufficient in another.

Show me the money

In the 1996 movie *Jerry Maguire* (1996), Rod Tidwell (played by Cuba Gooding Jr.) is a football player who feels undervalued by his team's management. During a pivotal conversation, he tells his agent, Jerry Maguire (played by Tom Cruise), that he wants him to demonstrate his commitment to him and encourages him to "show me the money." At the end of the day, while the reputation of the institution you work for and the quality of your colleagues and students are important, pay and benefits are significant considerations.

Other notable factors include the cost and quality of life where the educational institution is located. For example, a salary of $75,000 goes a lot further in Wichita, Kansas, than in New York City. And each part of a country has different cultures that may be a perfect fit for a candidate or may just be too alien for them, their partners, and dependents.

Is the university located in a college town, a large metropolitan area, the suburbs, or a rural setting? How far is the campus from your ideal living location, and do you need to reside nearby to access essential amenities such as specialized healthcare, public transportation, or shopping? Reflecting on these questions can help you make a more informed decision about the university where you are going to work and where you decide to live.

Also keep in mind that criminologists with earned doctorates will probably make more money and receive more benefits (e.g., retirement plans, educational support, etc.) working for a city/county (also known as local), state, or federal government agency than working as a professor for a university. They will also usually work a standard 9–5 workday, with weekends off. However, if you're an academic criminologist, the relative flexibility of the job often means preparing lectures, grading exams, and conducting research outside of standard work hours, including evenings and weekends.

Summing up

In conclusion, if you are interviewing for an instructional or faculty position in a criminology or criminal justice department, approach this task like a seasoned ethnographer. Ask thoughtful questions that probe the key themes discussed above and proceed with caution. Pay close attention not only to what is said, but also how, who said it and when it is said. Speak with a wide range of people, including faculty, administrators, and both undergraduate and graduate students. Look for patterns in their responses, as well as contradictions. Inconsistencies may reveal confusion, power imbalances, shifting policies and practices, or a culture of flexibility, all of which can have implications for your potential role.

Another point worth mentioning is that having the job title of a criminologist is like "the gift that keeps on giving." When people ask you what you do, you will forever have to explain what you do. In practice, most people don't have a clue what an academic criminologist does. Thus, you will encounter questions like "Are you a profiler or something like that?" Alternatively, "Do you help police catch bad guys?" These questions can be good conversation starters, but if you have to explain what you do in detail, you're more likely to encounter people quickly getting puzzled and/or bored. Or worse, thinking that you don't know what you are talking about.

Suggested reading

Gabbidon, S. L., & Higgins, G. E. (2012). The life of an academic: Examining the correlates of job satisfaction among Criminology/Criminal Justice faculty. *American Journal of Criminal Justice*, *37*(4), 669–681.

Gabbidon, S. L., Higgins, G. E., & Martin, F. (2011). Moving through the faculty ranks: An exploratory study on the perceived importance of book publishing and publishing in peer-reviewed journals in criminology/criminal justice. *Journal of Criminal Justice Education*, *22*(2), 165–180.

Koetzle, D. (2017). Assessing the quality of doctoral education (Mis) Counting who and what matters. *Journal of Criminal Justice Education*, *28*(4), 488–491.

Ross, J. I. (2005). On the road again: surviving the structural and procedural dynamics of interviewing for assistant professor jobs. *Professional Studies Review*, 2(1), 13–30.

Ross, J. I. (2007). Degrees R Us: Inside Cowtown U. *Professional Studies Review*, *3*(1), 103–128.

Letter 3

I HAVE A CRIMINAL RECORD AND/ OR WAS FORMERLY INCARCERATED. IS BEING AN ACADEMIC CRIMINOLOGIST A VIABLE CAREER OPTION FOR ME?

If earning a bachelor's, master's, and doctorate in criminology or a related field and pursuing an academic career at a university appeals to you, then the short answer is yes, it's a viable option. However, the path can be challenging, and understanding the requirements and potential obstacles, especially at the early stages of your educational journey, is essential.

Academic qualifications vs. lived experience

Many people with criminal records develop unique and valuable insights into crime, criminality, and the criminal justice system. This "lived experience" can provide powerful resources and perspectives that are relied upon, mainly when teaching or conducting research in criminology/criminal justice, especially when it concerns the prison system and reentry. However, it's important to recognize that personal experience alone does not equate to formal academic training.

To become an academic criminologist, you typically need to earn a doctorate in criminology, criminal justice, or a related discipline such as sociology, political science, or psychology (see the letter that addresses this issue). Then, you will need to develop a portfolio of scholarly publications. Although lived experience can complement academic expertise, a strong educational foundation is critical for securing a faculty position, conducting research, and teaching at the university level. Teaching undergraduate classes is also helpful, as this is the bread and butter of most criminology/ criminal justice academic careers.

DOI: 10.4324/9781003499145-5

It is also significant to understand the differences among people who are criminal justice system–contacted, criminal justice system–involved, and criminal justice system–impacted. There are subtle but important differences among these statuses (Ross, 2024, p. 4). And they can affect students' and instructors' approach to the study of and instruction of criminology and criminal justice.

Challenges for formerly incarcerated academics

Despite earning the necessary qualifications, people with criminal records often face significant difficulties in academia. Biases and misconceptions about individuals who have been convicted of crimes and incarcerated may exist and persist among departmental colleagues, students, and administrators. This is especially true for individuals who have been charged, convicted, and sentenced for sex-related crimes. Some may question whether someone with a criminal record should teach or conduct research in this field.

These prejudices can make it harder to secure an academic position, even for highly qualified candidates. Nevertheless, academic institutions need to embrace a 360-degree perspective of criminologists, one that includes voices from diverse backgrounds, including those directly impacted by the criminal justice system.

The role of convict criminology

For more than three decades, the convict criminology approach I co-founded has sought to address these challenges. Convict criminology emphasizes the value of lived experience in enriching the understanding of crime, justice, and corrections while advocating for greater inclusion within the discipline. This approach and praxis supports individuals with criminal records (including those who are criminal justice-contacted, involved, or impacted) earning advanced degrees while also working to dispel stereotypes the broader academic community may hold.

Overcoming obstacles and building a career as an academic criminologist

If you have a criminal record and aspire to become an academic criminologist, here are some steps to help navigate the path:

Don't assume or project an impression that you know everything: From arrest to conviction to sentencing to doing time, some formerly incarcerated people appear as if they know everything about crime, criminality, and criminal justice. This is truly not the case. Although lived experience is impactful, there is considerable diversity in individuals' experience of the criminal justice system; there is substantial scholarship that has been produced in these fields, and failure to acknowledge this reality is the downfall of many who are formally incarcerated or justice-impacted.

Pursue advanced education: Focus on completing your bachelor's, master's, and doctorate degrees in criminology, criminal justice, or a related discipline from a respected and accredited university. Academic credentials are essential for entering the field.

Build a strong publication record: Recognize the pecking order among different types of publications. Thus, attempt to publish articles in peer-reviewed journals to establish your credibility as a researcher. Sharing your unique insights through research can help counter biases and demonstrate your academic expertise.

Engage with convict criminology networks: Connect with scholars and organizations affiliated with convict criminology. These networks can provide mentorship, resources, and advocacy for their members.

Develop advocacy skills: Use your lived experience to advocate for criminal justice reform, whether through public speaking, teaching, or community engagement. This can enhance your profile as a scholar-practitioner.

Seek allies and mentors: Find appropriate mentors within academia (not necessarily at your university) who value diverse perspectives and can support your career development.

Demonstrate professionalism in all your interactions: Address potential biases by maintaining a professional demeanor and emphasizing your educational qualifications, research contributions, teaching ability, and professional service.

Final thoughts

Although becoming an academic criminologist can be more difficult for those with criminal records, it's not impossible. With determination, advanced education, strategic networking, and thoughtful consideration of academic norms and practices, it's possible to be hired by a respected department and for you to make significant contributions. Your lived experience, combined with formal academic training, can provide a richer, more nuanced understanding of criminology/criminal justice, one that benefits students, colleagues, research, and society as a whole.

Suggested reading

Connor, D. P., & Tewksbury, R. (2012). Ex-offenders and educational equal access: Doctoral programs in criminology and criminal justice. *Critical Criminology: An International Journal*, *20*(1), 327–340.

Ross, J. I. (2024). *Introduction to convict criminology*. Bristol University Press.

Ross, J. I., Richards, S. C., Newbold, G., Jones, R. S., Lenza, M., Murphy, D. S., Hogan, R. & Curry, G. D. (2011). Knocking on the ivory tower's door: The experience of Ex-convicts applying for tenure-track university positions. *Journal of Criminal Justice Education*, *22*(2), 267–285.

Tietjen, G., & Kavish, D. (2020). In the pool without a life jacket: Status fragility and convict criminology in the current criminological era. In J. I. Ross & F. Vianello (Eds.), *Convict criminology for the future* (pp. 66–82). Routledge.

Letter 4

ARE THE MAJORITY OF CRIMINOLOGISTS FORMER CRIMINALS OR CRIMINAL JUSTICE PRACTITIONERS?

A publicly available database that aggregates basic information on academic criminologists does not exist. Although I am unsure why this is the case, I suspect that creating one of these tools would require a considerable amount of resources, may run into privacy issues, and may be of questionable utility.

That said, what we can say with a high degree of confidence is that as of this current writing, the American Society of Criminology has approximately 4,000 members, while the Academy of Criminal Justice Sciences has about 1,800 members. This is followed by the British Society of Criminology with approximately 800 members; the Australian and New Zealand Society of Criminology with around 400 members, and the European Society of Criminology with about 1,000 members. These figures, however, should be understood as partial indicators, as they understate the global footprint of the discipline. Country-level criminology and criminal justice organizations exist across a wide range of national contexts, including throughout Latin America and East Asia.

Because criminologists don't need to register with these organizations or work for a college or university, the number of people in these learned societies is more like a snapshot. Also, many of these organizations do not disaggregate (i.e., statistically separate) students from professors or from those who work in government, the private, or nonprofit sectors. Thus, getting a reasonable estimate of the total number of criminologists in the world is difficult.

Criminologists who work in departments, schools, and colleges of criminology and criminal justice are usually diverse. However, the term "diverse"

DOI: 10.4324/9781003499145-6

means different things to different people. This variability is generally reflected in the educational background of instructional staff (i.e., the fields in which they earned their doctorate and the universities they attended), age, race/ethnicity, gender, national origin, religion, and sexual and political preferences. These elements contribute to making the discipline both interesting and sometimes challenging.

One of the more prominent distinctions among faculty, however, is their professional background. More specifically, what is their connection with the criminal justice system? This typically means whether they, close relatives, or a friend is or was a criminal justice practitioner, a perpetrator of one or more crimes, justice-contacted, justice-involved, justice-impacted, and/or a victim of a crime.

As other letters in this collection allude to, many former criminal justice professionals are now part-time or full-time instructional staff. Some are tenured, tenure-track, or adjuncts.

Ideally, instructional staff would approximate the racial, ethnic, and gender composition of their student bodies. Given that many students will enter criminal justice professions and work within demographically diverse communities, faculty diversity has clear pedagogical and professional relevance. Achieving this kind of balance, however, is constrained by structural and institutional factors, making it difficult to realize in practice.

For many years, departments of criminology and criminal justice were disproportionately staffed by white men. There was a shortage of women, minorities, and LGBTQ+ people working as criminologists at institutions of higher education. However, due to Affirmative Action laws passed in the 1960s and a realization by many that the field of criminology/criminal justice was suffering from a lack of diversity concerning the people teaching this material and the subject matter they researched, we needed to actively recruit new and diverse instructors and mentor them as junior faculty.

That said, some faculty subtly or overtly push their agendas, whether ideological, philosophical, political, methodological, etc. This approach to teaching and interpersonal relations may also involve biases of race, gender, or ethnicity. This is reflected not only in the courses criminologists teach, how they instruct these classes, research topics they may focus on, and their decisions about whom they wish to hire to join their department.

Increasingly, some departments have been open to hiring formerly incarcerated, justice-impacted, or system-impacted scholars. In fact, a surprising number of instructors have had some contact with the criminal justice system as a perpetrator of crime (Robinson & Zaitzow, 1999), a loved one who was incarcerated, or a victim of crime. These individuals often bring unique or nontraditional experiences to the study of criminology and criminal justice, which can be more realistic than those instructors who have spent only a fraction of their time directly in the field.

Then again, some criminologists appear to have neither been criminal justice practitioners nor have they been perpetrators, accomplices, the loved ones of people convicted, or even victims of crime. In many respects, they have spent most of their careers with their heads in the books (also known as in "the ivory tower").

What is the lesson here? The bottom line is that most departments of criminology or criminal justice include faculty and students with varying levels of direct experience with the criminal justice system; some may be former practitioners, others may have lived experience, and many have only academic exposure. This can be enriching, but it also creates potential for cultural clashes. Practitioners and those with lived experience may perceive others as naive or out of touch, which can strain professional relationships and negatively affect the working environment. Over time, such dynamics shape departmental cultures, making some places more inclusive and supportive than others for studying or working in the field.

Suggested reading

Custer, B. D., Malkin, M. L., & Castillo, G. (2020). Criminal justice system-impacted faculty: Motivations, barriers, and successes on the academic job market. *Journal of Education Human Resources*, *38*(2), 336–364.

Robinson, M. B., & Zaitzow, B. H. (1999, March/April). Criminologists: Are we what we study? A national self-report study of crime experts. *The Criminologist*, *24*(3), 17–19.

Letter 5

ARE MOST ACADEMIC DEPARTMENTS, SCHOOLS, AND COLLEGES OF CRIMINOLOGY OR CRIMINAL JUSTICE SO-CALLED "COP SHOPS"?[1]

Many academic departments (schools and colleges) of criminology and criminal justice, at least in the United States, are often disparagingly called "cop shops." What does this mean? This label is frequently affixed to academic units that are disproportionately staffed by instructors and professors who are former criminal justice practitioners or professionals, and there is a belief that this situation negatively affects pedagogy, scholarship, and organizational culture. Let's examine this claim a little more closely.

Although learned organizations like the American Society of Criminology (ASC) and the Academy of Criminal Justice Sciences (ACJS) ask their members to indicate where they work and their highest level of education, as previously mentioned, no publicly available database contains statistics about the careers or professional backgrounds of the instructors and professors who work as criminology and criminal justice instructors or professors.

Also, given the frequency of the cop shop complaints, with the exceptions of a scholarly article by Garner and Lyons (2016) and Johnson's (2012) edited book on correctional professionals who have transitioned to academic jobs, it's somewhat perplexing that hardly any scholarship has been produced that examines this issue.

So much of what follows is, thus, personal and based on my impressions.

My history

Before diving deeper into answering this question, and in the spirit of fuller disclosure, many years ago, I worked for almost four years in a correctional facility. Furthermore, only a handful of the full-time faculty (i.e., professors) in the criminology/criminal justice departments I've worked in have

DOI: 10.4324/9781003499145-7

had practitioner experience. More typically throughout the United States, many adjuncts or part-timers in criminology/criminal justice departments are current or former professionals (many with master's degrees only).

With that in mind, in the distant past, when I was applying for assistant professor jobs, some of the departments of criminology/criminal justice where I interviewed were what most of my colleagues and I would probably call cop shops. Although a handful of the faculty earned their doctorates in criminology/criminal justice or allied fields, many of the full-time instructional staff had earned their PhDs in the discipline of education, typically holding an *EdD* (*Doctor of Education*). Moreover, the full-time faculty produced very few academic publications. On a related note, the departments, schools, or colleges of criminology/criminal justice that are often called cop shops rarely have a PhD program but more than likely stop their degree offerings with a terminal master's degree.

Understanding nuance

In reality, there are many different models or mixes concerning the percentage of full-time faculty who have practitioner experience, and the effect of this reality on pedagogy, scholarship, and organizational culture is varied. Someone (if suitably motivated) could develop a heuristic to rank departments based on how many former police and correctional officers they employ, at what academic rank, etc. Alternatively, some classes (e.g., "Introduction to Policing," or "Introduction to Corrections," Courts, Criminal Law, etc.) lend themselves better than others to being taught by former practitioners, whereas others (e.g., "Criminological Theory," "Research Methods," etc.) might be tackled better by people who have earned traditional doctorates.

Predictably, many ex-practitioners work (at all employment levels) in departments, schools, and colleges of criminology/criminal justice. These professionals are knowledgeable about the scholarly literature, teach, and conduct nuanced and thoughtful research, sometimes more so than that generated by their liberal and critical colleagues. These ex-professionals may even be better academic citizens than most instructors and professors in their departments.

Why do cop shop departments exist?

Introduction

Although community colleges seem to have more current and former practitioners working as instructors than universities, there are about four interrelated reasons why a university department of criminology/criminal justice may employ an abundance of individuals teaching with practitioner experience.

Size of department

Although anomalies exist, in principle, the bigger the department (in terms of students, faculty, and staff), the greater the possibility that one or more instructors/professors will have practitioner experience.

Historical legacy

Some of the cop shop legacy more than likely was aided and abetted by the U.S. Department of Justice, Law Enforcement Assistance Administration (1968–1982) funding, which offered practitioners grants or loans to pursue master's degrees and doctorates. With each new hire, the faculty working in criminology/criminal justice academic units and the senior leadership at those universities developed higher expectations, often demanding publications surpassing those of any single faculty member and occasionally exceeding the entire instructional staff combined. As a result, those hired have frequently heard stories of hostile work environments and a clash of cultures.

The power of geographic location

The designation of specific academic units as "cop shops" is influenced not only by the department's size and history, but also by geographic factors. Some criminology/criminal justice instructors may avoid living or working in certain cities or regions due to inadequate compensation at local institutions, high cost of living, challenges in raising a family, or personal dislike of the local culture. Consequently, these areas may struggle to attract traditional academics, leading to a higher proportion of former and current practitioners in the employment pool.

The dynamics of supply and demand

For a variety of reasons, many practitioners earn not just bachelor's degrees but also master's and doctorates. These degrees are frequently earned in the fields of criminology and criminal justice, the motivations for doing so vary widely. In most cases, an advanced degree, regardless of the discipline is the price of admission to teaching at a community college or university.

It may be challenging to recruit a qualified PhD candidate for some cities or regions in the country, so the former chief of police of a small town, who earned a Doctor of Education (EdD), gets the position because few candidates want to work there.

Advantages and disadvantages of having departments staffed by former practitioners

Overall, few scholars, instructors, or professors would dispute the value of practical experience in shaping effective pedagogy. In fact, instruction, especially in fields where students aspire to become practitioners, can be more grounded, relevant, realistic, and practical when delivered by those with direct professional experience.

Meanwhile, the hope exists that, despite its possible entertainment value, instruction in this field isn't dominated by anecdotal experiences (e.g., war stories and discussions on the best way to handcuff suspects) but also encourages a thoughtful, balanced discussion of the empirical evidence accumulated in criminology/criminal justice. Also, it's necessary to remember that there is an underlying belief that "lived experiences" can potentially inform an instructor's ability to make sense of the empirical knowledge related to the profession.

Some academics, including criminologists with prior experience as practitioners, may be able to assist students in finding jobs within the field. However, their effectiveness depends on their willingness to help, the strength of their professional connections, and how long they have been out of practice. Those who have been away from the profession for many years may be less helpful as hiring practices and industry standards evolve, and networks fade.

One more thing... A tendency to call a department a cop shop might derive from an "elitist" point of view. Those doing the labeling may believe that former practitioners are too basic (or conservative) in what they consider to be the necessary issues in the discipline of criminology/criminal justice and that instructors with doctorates in criminology/criminal justice (and a bunch of scholarly publications to their name) have not been tainted by this practitioner experience. Depending on the level of interaction, interaction with former practitioners might be hostile.

Here is the rub

If a department of criminology/criminal justice is willing to hire former law enforcement, correctional, and probation/parole officers and administrators, not to mention criminal lawyers, then it should also be open to employing formerly incarcerated individuals with doctorates (see previous letter "I have a criminal record and/or was formerly incarcerated. Is being an academic criminologist a viable career option for me?"). I'm not suggesting that this will be a panacea or some magic bullet to achieve the inclusivity of different voices in the curriculum. However, it might provide an alternative to the current ethos. This is perhaps why, over the past few years, an increasing number of criminology/criminal justice departments have hired instructors specializing in convict criminology.

For my colleagues without practitioner experience who get jobs in cop shop departments, it's entirely possible that these environments are supportive and that their former law enforcement department members are super friendly and very engaged with students, the subject matter, and the profession. However, if interactions with these people are hostile, then, depending on how much interaction they have with you, the experience may be challenging Also, it is important to take into consideration that some departments may be dominated by individuals with strong activist orientations (e.g., prison abolition, restorative justice, etc.) whose presence can heavily influence departmental dynamics and discussions.

Unfortunately, the "cop shop" designation has discouraged some prospective doctoral students from pursuing criminology/criminal justice and has deterred many PhD holders from working in such departments. As a result, some seek positions in allied fields such as sociology, political science, or public policy, where they anticipate a better disciplinary and organizational fit. This underscores the importance of understanding disciplinary boundaries, however fluid they may be, but also departmental culture when evaluating academic career paths.

All this is to say that students can get a respectable education in cop shop departments, and criminologists without criminal justice practitioner experience can have a satisfactory career in one of these work environments, too. Nonetheless, it's significant to understand the backgrounds of potential colleagues, the department's dynamics and culture, and the factors that shape them.

Note

1 An earlier version of this letter was published as "Are mostacademic departments, schools, and colleges of criminology or criminal justicecop shops?" March 11, 2024. https://jeffreyianross.com/are-most-academic-departments-schools-and-colleges-of-criminology-or-criminal-justice-cop-shops/

Suggested reading

Garner, R., & Lyons, P. (2016). In defense of "cop shop" pedagogy. *Applied Psychology in Criminal Justice, 12*(2), 126–132.

Johnson, L. M. (Ed.). (2012). *Experiencing corrections: From practitioner to professor*. Sage Publications.

Letter 6

DO OTHER SOCIAL SCIENCE DISCIPLINES LOOK DOWN ON CRIMINOLOGY/CRIMINAL JUSTICE?

Many academics have a habit of comparing themselves based on the universities from which they earned their doctorates, the disciplines in which they earned their degrees, and the ones in which they currently work. That being said, over the years, I've heard numerous disparaging comments directed against not just the academic fields of criminology and criminal justice, but also the people who work in them. There are multiple reasons why this occurs.

First, *jealousy* may motivate this behavior. Colleagues in cognate disciplines (e.g., law, political science, psychology, sociology, etc.) may feel that criminologists receive the same or better compensation for less effort or possess less talent. Whether justified or not, this perception often leads to resentment, especially when disparities in workload and compensation are suspected between departments. Such feelings can exacerbate tensions, fostering a competitive atmosphere where comparisons and insecurities shape professional relationships and behavior.

Second, occasionally, highly judgmental attitudes toward the discipline of criminology are motivated by *insecurity*. Just like children complaining to their parents that their siblings got an extra helping of dessert, grown adults with doctorates in allied fields may feel that criminologists do not deserve the same compensation and benefits as they do.

Third, some instructors in departments of criminology/criminal justice and the students who enroll in their classes are *mediocre and lazy*. The teaching staff struggled as students, but some eventually became instructors and professors. The fact that many departments of criminology and criminal justice are or appear to be cop shops does not help the field's reputation.

DOI: 10.4324/9781003499145-8

Fourth, there is a perception that the academic disciplines of criminology and criminal justice have *lower academic standards* and are, thus, easy majors. If you cannot get accepted into other, more traditional social science departments, the belief is that you can always get into a department of criminology/criminal justice.

Fifth, the views about how *demanding* an academic field like criminology/criminal justice inevitably vary based on the college, university, region, etc. It's not uncommon for professors at universities that are relatively close in proximity to refer to professors at the other university as substandard. This isn't a matter of the grass being greener on the other side (although it might be). This is a justification of why they are here and not there.

Sixth, negative views directed toward the field of criminology/criminal justice (and the people who work in that discipline) may also be connected to criminology's being characterized as a *rendezvous discipline* (i.e., one that sits at the crossroads of various interrelated fields).

Seventh, some liberals, progressives, and activists (both inside and outside of the academy) argue that *criminologists are complicit in sustaining the criminal justice–industrial complex*, the web of public and private entities that reinforce criminal justice institutions as the primary response to crime and social deviance, often for financial gain. In the meantime, they believe that their work remains independent, untainted by government or corporate funding. Yet such a stance overlooks the broader structural entanglements of academia with state power and financial interests, making claims of intellectual purity difficult to sustain. More about this later.

This sense of negativity, real or imagined, leads to protectionism, manifesting in the reluctance of some criminal justice and criminology departments to hire people who have not earned their PhD in criminology/criminal justice. For example, some schools refuse to consider hiring those with sociology doctorates, even if they have a concentration in criminology/criminal justice, and even if many of the older faculty hold sociology degrees. As you can probably assume, criminal justice, criminology, and sociology folks all stereotype each other. This may also extend to a reluctance to hire people trained as lawyers (JDs) (more about this later), unless they have an earned PhD at least as tenure-line faculty.

In the end, it's important to be mindful of this mindset and practice but also to abandon this approach and focus on more significant things, like being a good instructor and mentor, doing meaningful service to your educational institution and the profession, and conducting significant research that has a positive impact.

Suggested reading

Akers, R. L. (1992). Linking sociology and its specialties: The case of criminology. *Social Forces*, *71*(1), 1–16.

Wrede, C., & Featherstone, R. (2012). Striking out on its own: The divergence of criminology and criminal justice from sociology. *Journal of Criminal Justice Education*, *23*(1), 103–125.

Letter 7

WHAT IS THE DIFFERENCE BETWEEN CRIMINOLOGISTS WHO WORK FOR COMMUNITY COLLEGES AND THOSE WHO WORK FOR UNIVERSITIES?[1]

Although some high schools offer courses in criminology and/or criminal justice, instruction in these fields usually occurs at community colleges and universities.[2] In the United States and Canada, community colleges typically offer programs for students wishing to achieve some sort of technical or practitioner/applied expertise (e.g., dental technician, draftsman, etc.).

On the other hand, universities have professional schools (e.g., architecture, dentistry, law, medicine, etc.) and usually liberal arts education. Admission to community colleges generally requires high school graduation or a General Equivalency Diploma (U.S.). In contrast, entrance into universities is more competitive. It requires not only a minimum grade point average (GPA) but often an acceptable score on a standardized performance test like the Scholastic Assessment Test (SAT).

Although I've never attended or taught criminology/criminal justice at a community college, I've participated in a handful of joint day-long events with instructors and administrators working at these institutions. I've also had numerous conversations with fellow criminologists who either work or used to work at these types of schools.

Community colleges and universities differ on about six critical criteria: Organization, resources, instructors, students, teaching methods and evaluation, and remuneration. Complicating these issues are the expectations of various parties involved. These are discussed below from least to most important.

DOI: 10.4324/9781003499145-9

Organizational setup

Unlike many universities, the student bodies at most community colleges are primarily commuter in nature; students drive or take public transportation to the campus, and they go home. In other words, the campus rarely has residential dormitories, whereas big state universities typically provide student housing. Community college students tend to attend classes for two years and graduate with an associate's degree. There may also be a proliferation of certificate courses at a community college. Lastly, criminology/criminal justice departments at such institutions may fall under a broader umbrella of public safety instruction and may include fire and emergency medical services fields. In the United States, some states (e.g., North Carolina, Maryland, etc.) have established networks or consortia of community college criminal justice educators. These instructors and professors share job-related information, meet periodically, and may even have an annual one-day conference where they bring practitioners in and have students make presentations at these venues.

Do the resources differ between community colleges and universities?

When we talk about resources, we typically mean remuneration and benefits. It's well known that instructors at community colleges typically earn less than their counterparts at universities. However, in some cases, strong faculty unions at community colleges have negotiated salaries and benefits that rival or even exceed those at some universities. This is especially true where union contracts are strong, and there is considerable solidarity amongst the workers, while university faculty pay can vary widely depending on rank, discipline, and union strength.

Other resources may be less obvious (e.g., a parking spot). Unlike universities, there is a lot more top-down administrative control of criminology/criminal justice programs at community colleges. This includes control over the curriculum. Instructors walking into a job at a community college may be presented with a syllabus by their chair, and they are told that this is what and how they will be teaching that semester. For some teaching staff, this is a little off-putting; for others, it may mean the decision about what text to assign has already been handled by the school, and it temporarily makes things easier for them.

What is the difference between instructors working in community colleges and those working at universities?

Instructors at community colleges generally have a master's degree, are less likely to have earned a PhD, and may not necessarily have practitioner experience in the subjects they teach. Instructors are rarely required to conduct research to rise through the ranks or earn permanent status at community colleges. And if instructors do research, then it's seen as anomalous. If they had once worked in their discipline, they may have been employed as correctional, probation, parole, police officers, or social workers. Additionally, a community college might have a lot of JDs and LLBs on staff. And many of the master's degrees that these individuals earned are in the field of education, where they only needed to take comprehensive exams or complete a significant project to graduate, not a thesis. A position at a community college might be a good job for an all-but-dissertation (ABD) student. Likewise, community colleges often employ individuals whose PhD studies were interrupted reflecting broader patterns of doctoral attrition and academic labor market constraints.

Who are your students?

College students come from diverse backgrounds; some enroll right after high school, while others are already working in the criminal justice field and pursuing further education. Many criminal justice majors aim for careers in law enforcement, corrections, or related professions.

Students who enroll in and take courses at community colleges differ slightly from those who attend universities. Universities may require prospective students to achieve a specific score on a standardized test (e.g., the SAT) for admission or to maintain a higher grade point average than students entering community colleges. Many community colleges also have transfer or articulation agreements with traditional local or regional universities.

> The articulation agreement allows the students, who have... completed a required general education set of courses that culminates with an associate degree, to automatically be admitted into the four-year school as an upper-division student. All of the general education courses and usually a few of the students' major courses are credited toward their bachelor's degree. (Hartman et al., 2009, p. 176)

It's not uncommon for approximately 31-33% of the students who graduate from community college programs to then go on to university.

Most students in both settings have professional aspirations to work in the criminal justice system. Many students at the community college level want to work in law enforcement, probation and parole, or victim services, including battered women's shelters. There is also a tendency for students at community colleges to have working-class backgrounds, and they may be more conservative, tough on crime, and punitive in their attitudes toward lawbreakers, including criminals, than their university student counterparts.

They are also less likely to be critical thinkers than students who have enrolled in universities.

In university settings, although many of your students will want to be law enforcement, probation, and parole officers, some of them will also aspire to be lawyers.

Are teaching methods different or the same in community colleges versus at universities?

Many instructors with doctoral degrees who teach at community colleges may feel as if they have to “dumb down” the material that they teach their students. They may also find it impractical to teach about criminological theory and criminal justice policy and concentrate more on practical things like internships, placements, etc. Teachers at community colleges are frequently given a set syllabus, which includes a required textbook that must be used. Thus, there is rarely intellectual freedom regarding what an instructor can teach. In short, intellectual variety is hampered in this context. Just like universities, and increasingly because of COVID-19 restrictions and competition for students among community colleges, there has been an increase in online and hybrid teaching. There may also be many accessible, applied, and practical learning opportunities at the community college level. This might include mock court labs and perhaps smaller classrooms with 30–60 students per class. Also, unlike some university settings, community colleges do not use teaching assistants. Although this practice can vary among universities, there may be more interaction between instructors and students in community college settings than in a university setting. There may also be more first-generation students at community colleges than at universities.

Are the methods of evaluation in community colleges different?

The way instructors evaluate students differs between the two types of institutions. Community college instructors typically evaluate their students using multiple-choice, short answer and fill-in-the-blank tests. There may also be less essay type requirements then those used in university settings.

Wrapping up

In summary, working at a community college significantly differs from working as a criminologist at a university. But there are lots of advantages. The pressure to publish and do lots of mindless and soul-crushing service is just not there. It forces you to apply the knowledge you acquired during your university training and apply what you know to the people who are most likely working as practitioners in field.

Notes

1 Special thanks to Denis Lim, Stephen Muzzatti, and Emma Smith for sharing their experiences with me.
2 Some technical colleges, such as Albany Technical College, Central Georgia Technical College, Fayetteville Technical Community College, Fox Valley Technical College, Gwinnett Technical College, and Lake Area Technical College, offer criminology/criminal justice programs.

Suggested reading

Lumb, R. C., & Alm, M. (1986). High-quality criminal justice education and the role of the community college. *American Journal of Criminal Justice*, *11*(1), 38–46.

Wallace, L. N. (2022). Criminal justice students' perceptions of their future careers. *Journal of Criminal Justice Education, 34*(2), 169–184.

Letter 8

DOES THE ACADEMIC FIELD OF CRIMINOLOGY/CRIMINAL JUSTICE PROMOTE DIVERSITY, EQUITY, AND INCLUSION IN HIRING, PROMOTION, RESEARCH, AND TEACHING PRACTICES?

Once a predominantly white and male academic discipline, criminology and criminal justice has been gradually becoming more diverse in terms of the racial, ethnic, and gender backgrounds of those earning doctorates, securing faculty positions, publishing in respected journals, the content of research, and holding leadership roles in our learned societies.

There are numerous reasons why the field was white and male-dominated, and I suspect that it had a lot to do with the fact that many early criminologists were former criminal justice practitioners and that old white men dominated this profession. Thus, their teaching, research, and writing reflected their gender, ethnic, and racial backgrounds, not to mention the implications for who they accepted into master's and PhD programs, who graduated, and whom they hired into the hallowed halls of academe.

That being said, a substantial minority of historically black universities and colleges (HBCUs) have their own criminology/criminal justice departments, schools, and colleges. They have bachelor's, master's, and some doctoral degrees. Two in particular (i.e., Southern Methodist University (Houston) and Prairie View University) have dedicated PhD programs in criminology/criminal justice. And as I implied earlier, if you can't pursue a doctoral degree specifically in criminology/criminal justice at an HBCU, it does not mean you can't enroll in and complete a PhD in an allied field.

However, many changes have occurred since the 1960s, not just in academic departments of criminology/criminal justice but throughout institutions of higher education. These include, but are not limited to, affirmative action legislation, regulations, policies, and practices, and the gradual and

DOI: 10.4324/9781003499145-10

increasing acceptance of women, African Americans, and Hispanics into fields that were traditionally closed to them.

Merlo (2016), for example, writes,

> Twenty or thirty years ago, the discipline of criminology and criminal justice was male-oriented. That has changed. In the 2014 survey of the Association of Doctoral Programs in Criminology and Criminal Justice survey of 39 doctoral programs, female doctoral students comprised 58% of the 1,363 doctoral students (ADPCCJ, 2014, p. 10), and increasingly, academic departments are more balanced in terms of gender. There has been tremendous progress in academic departments, and the data indicate more equal representation of men and women in 2015–2016 than in previous generations. (p. 187)

Part of this change is reflected in the American Society of Criminology and the Academy of Criminal Justice Sciences. Both learned societies include divisions dedicated to advancing the interests of underrepresented communities and fostering scholarship that promotes these constituencies.[1] Moreover, many of the key ASC and ACJS committees are composed if not led by, of members from diverse demographic backgrounds.

We also see more women, and LGBTQ+ people, of all races and ethnicities as students, instructors, and leaders in our academic institutions and our criminology/criminal justice learned organizations. Nevertheless, the ASC has only had two African American Presidents (Ruth Peterson, 2015–2016 and Kathryn Russell Brown, 2024–2025). The same cannot be said of the Academy of Criminal Justice Sciences. It is more common to see visible minorities in the regional criminal justice learned societies (e.g., Southwestern, Northeastern, and Midwestern Criminal Justice Associations).

The issue of diversity and inclusiveness has been raised in our learned organizations and the annual conferences (Panfil & Cobbina-Dungy, 2023) we attend. In 2020, a study was commissioned by the executive of the ASC. To begin with, "Participants from minoritized groups experienced inclusion by seeing diversity in leadership positions within ASC, ASC Divisions, other major roles, as well as mentoring and networking" (p. 9). The researchers also found a considerable number of women, scholars of color, LGBTQ+, and formerly incarcerated individuals who experienced instances of alienation, disrespect, othering, etc. In this same vein, "disabled people... [felt] excluded due to issues of physical mobility, hearing and visual impairments, and off-site events" (p. 8). "Focus group and interview participants expressed disappointment that no clear, articulated policy and processes existed for reporting, investigating, and accountability and sanctions" (p. 9).

Diversity, should not be limited to race and ethnicity. It must also include religion, gender, national origin, age, and individuals with lived experience in the criminal justice system, an aspect that is too often overlooked or misunderstood by many people and organizations.

Clearly, more needs to be done to make the academic field of criminology/criminal justice more inclusive. This is going to be even more difficult during the second Trump Administration, which is rolling back DEI initiatives and protections.

Note

1 The ASC has the Division of Convict Criminology, Division of Feminist Criminology, Division of People of Color and Crime, Division on Queer Criminology, and the ACJS has the Minorities and Women Section.

Suggested reading

Bernat, F. P. (2022). Diversity in teaching and researching criminal law and criminology. In D. M. D. Silva & M. Deflem (Eds.), Diversity in criminology and criminal justice studies (pp. 9–23). Emerald Publishing Limited.

Chesney-Lind, M., & Chagnon, N. (2016). Criminology, gender, and race: A case study of privilege in the academy. *Feminist Criminology*, *11*(4), 311–333.

Fahmy, C., & Young, J. T. N. (2017). Gender inequality and knowledge production in criminology and criminal justice. *Journal of Criminal Justice Education*, *28*(2), 285–305.

Gilbert, E., & Tatum, B. L. (1999). African American women in the criminal justice academy: Characteristics, perceptions, and coping strategies. *Journal of Criminal Justice Education*, *10*(2), 231–246.

Glispie, S. (2012). African American perceptions of graduate school experiences and employment in criminal justice and criminology. *McNair Scholarly Review*, *18*(1), 23–33.

Greene, H. T., Gabbidon, S. L., & Wilson, S. K. (2018). Included? The status of African American scholars in the discipline of criminology and criminal justice since 2004. *Journal of Criminal Justice Education*, *29*(1), 96–115.

Merlo, A. V. (2016). The pre-tenure years: Survive, succeed, and thrive. *Journal of Criminal Justice Education*, *27*(2), 175–193.

Moton, L., & Blount-Hill, K. L. (2022). Inclusive criminology: Embracing a comprehensive scope of the discipline. *The Criminologist*, *49*(2), 1, 3–7.

Panfil, V., & Cobbina-Dungy, J. (2023). Improving the climate at ASC meetings and sponsored events: Insights from attendees and actions taken by ASC leadership. *The Criminologist*, 49(5), 8–11.

Potter, H., Higgins, G. E., & Gabbidon, S. L. (2011). The influence of gender, race/ethnicity, and faculty perceptions on scholarly productivity in criminology/criminal justice. *Journal of Criminal Justice Education*, *22*(1), 84–101.

Sever, B., Rolland, S., & Fabrizio, C. (2024). Faculty demographics in criminology and criminal justice: A wider view. *Journal of Criminal Justice Education*, 36(4),784–804.

Stockdale, K. J., & Sweeney, R. (2022). Whose voices are prioritized in criminology, and why does it matter? *Race and Justice*, *12*(3), 481–504.

Toro-Pascua, J. C., & Martín-González, Y. (2022). Presence of women on the editorial boards of criminology journals. *Journal of Criminal Justice Education*, *33*(4), 491–508.

Walker, A., Valcore, J., Evans, B., & Stephens, A. (2021). Experiences of trans scholars in criminology and criminal justice. *Critical Criminology: An International Journal*, *29*(1), 37–56.

Letter 9

WHAT DO CRIMINOLOGISTS WEAR?[1]

Growing up, my friend Mark (not his real name) shared a story about applying for a summer job at Switzer's Delicatessen on Spadina Avenue (Toronto). Following advice from his friends, or perhaps his mother, he donned the only suit he owned, a slightly ill-fitting one, took the TTC (Toronto's public transportation system) to the deli, and introduced himself to the owner with the firmest handshake he could muster.

The owner gave him a quick once-over and said, "If you're going to work here, you can't be dressed in a suit, and you'd better be ready to get your clothes dirty."

Similarly, when I worked in a correctional facility, staff and inmates were encouraged to wear street clothing. This flexibility in dress code sometimes led detainees to ask me what crime I was in for, a question I might not have encountered if I'd been dressed more formally.

These experiences highlight how clothing influences our interactions and perceptions in professional settings. Whether for a job interview, working in a criminal justice agency, or teaching in a classroom, attire is more than just fabric; it communicates authority, identity, and intention.

The role of clothing in professional contexts

My early lessons about the effect of clothing on different audiences resurfaced recently when I was browsing at a local bookstore in Washington, DC (yes, a few of them still exist). I stumbled upon a book titled *What Artists Wear?* and couldn't help but wonder: Is there anything special about the clothes that criminologists wear?

DOI: 10.4324/9781003499145-11

Although criminologists' clothing isn't particularly unique compared to other social scientists, it does play an essential role in shaping perceptions.

Even though I'm neither an expert on fashion nor style, my experience in street ethnography has sensitized me to how clothing can influence perception and interaction.

For example, when I started my first assistant professor job, determined to project a professional image, I wore a suit and tie for the entire first week. But it didn't take long to realize I was overdressed for the role. Over time, I transitioned to a more personal "uniform": A black T-shirt, black jeans, and black cowboy or biker boots, a subtle nod to Johnny Cash. I also grew my hair into a shoulder-length ponytail and, for a while, sported a collection of earrings and an ear cuff.

This evolution wasn't just about comfort; it reflected a quiet rebellion against rigid academic expectations and a growing confidence in my identity. Had I kept that look today, I might have been mistaken for an aging biker or hippie. But in academia, such casual dressing walks a fine line: It might suggest brilliance and boldness, or simply that it's laundry day.

Understandably, the factors shaping clothing choices and their interpretations are not uniform. What we wear, when and where we wear it, how we choose to wear it, and how others perceive us are deeply influenced by gender norms, age, financial resources, cultural and regional practices, disciplinary orientation, and the specific setting, all play a role in what we wear and how others perceive us.

Gendered effects

In most Western academic settings, men face less scrutiny for their appearance. A male professor in worn jeans and a wrinkled shirt rarely draws a comment. A woman academic dressed identically appears unprofessional. Women navigate broader clothing options but narrower tolerance for missteps. Students, colleagues, and administrators evaluate them not just on professionalism but on attractiveness, age-appropriateness, and conformity to feminine norms they may not share. Trans and gender nonconforming students, instructors, and professors may find it especially difficult to operate in settings where criminologists are present. And they must negotiate their choices of clothing more carefully among students, colleagues, and administrators.

Generational components

Generational factors also influence clothing choices. Older professionals are generally not expected to dress like people in their 20s, and defying these norms can draw attention. For academics, balancing professionalism with individuality often involves navigating these generational expectations.

Money talks

Financial considerations are another critical factor. While most tenured professors will be able to afford a decent set of duds, adjunct instructors often lack the resources to dress professionally, let alone feed, clothe, and house themselves and their loved ones. This disparity underscores broader inequities not just in the field of criminology/criminal justice but in academia more generally.

Regional and cultural differences

Regional and cultural differences also exist in how academics (criminologists or otherwise) dress. For example, when I attended the University of Toronto, no self-respecting male professor would come to class without a suit and tie (or equivalent professional outfit for women). However, when I moved to the United States to start graduate school (at the University of Colorado), I was surprised by professors wearing more casual clothing, such as shorts and Birkenstocks.

Dressing for the occasion

Context is crucial when choosing what to wear. Criminologists, like other professionals, should consider their audience and the setting. Their attire tends to vary in three primary contexts: The classroom, conferences, and fieldwork.

Teaching mode

If I'm teaching and want to present myself professionally to students, colleagues, and staff, I dress business casual, neat, and put-together without overdoing it. This doesn't mean I wear a suit and tie, but a polo or button-down shirt and neatly pressed jeans, khakis, or chinos will suffice. On the rare occasions I wear a suit to class, usually because I've an important meeting before or after, it raises eyebrows among students, colleagues, and staff. It engenders comments like "What's up?" "Did you get a raise?" or "You're looking more professional today."

Conference participation

At academic annual meetings, and depending on your role (i.e., presenter, audience member, etc.), the appropriate attire can vary. For instance, as a presenter, I dress more professionally (usually business formal to business casual). It's also common to wear more formal clothing on the day of your presentation and then dress more casually on the other days or in the evenings. Finding the right balance can be tricky, but it gets easier with experience.

That being said, many European male criminologists dress with more style than their American counterparts, often adopting a "smart casual" or "business casual with a European twist" look. This style, also called "Continental Smart Casual," typically features a dark blazer or suit jacket, a white dress shirt, and jeans (but no tie). This approach embodies understated sophistication that is polished yet less rigid than a full suit. (Think of brands like Club Monaco, COS, Massimo Dutti, etc.) Some of my male colleagues can even rock a 5 o'clock shadow 24 hours a day, a skill I've yet to perfect, but I am working on it. Similarly, many female criminologists embrace a smart casual look, sometimes incorporating tailored skirts or dresses that complement this style's professional yet relaxed ethos. (Consider brands like Club Monaco, Massimo Dutti, rag & bone, Sandro, Theory, etc.) That said, it's sometimes amusing to see how uncomfortable some attendees, regardless of their chosen style, seem in their professional attire. They wear ill-fitting suits or ones that need to be properly tailored. They didn't know or care that to look better in the suits that they needed to be tailored.

Fieldwork clothing

The most significant variation in attire occurs when criminologists conduct fieldwork. For instance, when visiting a prison, I usually wear a suit or business casual clothing to convey professionalism and respect for both the environment and the individuals I engage with.

Conversely, when conducting street ethnography, which may include observing and speaking with graffiti writers or street artists, I opt for casual, nonthreatening street clothes (not streetwear) that are comfortable and appropriate for the setting. (A sturdy pair of running shoes also comes in handy if I ever need to high-tail it out of a dodgy situation.)

Other issues to consider

Disciplinary orientation

Another source of variation in clothing style may also be related to disciplinary orientation. For example, a former criminal justice practitioner turned university professor or a person working in a so-called "cop shop" may be more professional in their attire. Meanwhile, critical criminologists may dress more casually/rebelliously, opting for torn jeans, etc. Then again, criminologists who are more interested in policy might dress more conservatively (their clothing brands of choice might include Brooks Brothers, Hickey Freeman, etc.).

Exploring identity

Attire also serves as a medium for self-expression. For some criminologists, clothing isn't just functional but a way to infuse individuality and creativity into their professional lives. Accessories like tattoos or body modifications (earrings and where they are placed), and hairstyles (wildly multicolored dyed hair) may further reflect this blending of personal and professional identities.

Tailoring attire to the situation

From integrating into research settings to commanding respect in the classroom or projecting credibility at conferences, attire plays a crucial role for criminologists. Beyond selecting research topics, analyzing data, and communicating ideas to students and colleagues, decisions about what to wear are essential in academic and professional life. Just like deciding what subject to conduct research on, which journal to submit a paper to, the clothes that criminologists wear are important considerations in one's career in this field.

Note

1 An earlier version of this letter appeared as "What Do Criminologists Wear?"December 14, 2024. https://jeffreyianross.com/what-do-criminologists-wear/ (Download July 29, 2025).

Letter 10

HOW SHOULD CRIMINOLOGISTS DECORATE THEIR OFFICES?

Academic offices come in all shapes and sizes. Some resemble sleek executive suites, while others are the dreaded open style featured in Hollywood movies like *Wall Street*. As graduate students, we dreamed of having our own office. However, there was a pecking order from the bullpen office with dividers to the shared office (typically converted dormitory rooms located in the basement of an academic building). If you had an appointment as a researcher working for a professor or were a teaching assistant, you stood a greater chance of having an office, but this was on a semester-to-semester basis.

As a professor teaching at a public university in the United States, I know the situation is sometimes no better. Consider yourself lucky if you have your own office. However, be careful of converted broom closets or utility rooms with cockroaches, rats, mice, mold, poor air quality, no windows, and asbestos.

Why have an office?

Offices for professors serve numerous functions. They are places where you can do your research, prepare or review your lectures or classes, grade exams, quizzes, or essays, or meet students and colleagues. There are also rooms where you can temporarily hide from your students, chairs, colleagues, partners, and perhaps your kids. If you have a serious drinking problem or drug addiction or are sleep-deprived, then having your own office is a "safe space" where you can imbibe, trip out, or zone out for a few hours with little chance of being disturbed. If you have a couch, then you may be able to catch a few winks while in a prone position.

DOI: 10.4324/9781003499145-12

Location of the office

However, if the bulk of your research is off-site (e.g., in the field or at the library), an office on campus is redundant. Alternatively, your office may be on the other side of campus. This situation has its advantages and disadvantages. While you may risk being late to your lectures, it's a convenient way to get your steps in. Also, since your office is comparatively remote, there is a greater chance that all but the brave will visit you. As professors, we are required to include office hours in our syllabus, a relic of a bygone era. However, you will have few visitors if your office is relatively remote.

As a beginning professor, it may be hard not to think you're like the lonely Maytag repairman featured in television commercials where no one comes to your office. That said, I once had an office (not in an academic setting, mind you) that co-workers had difficulty finding. It was hidden behind an elevator shaft on the top floor of a building. Despite the constant whirring sound of the motors in the hydraulic system that I could successfully tune out if I played music loudly, it was a blessing in disguise. No one would drop in on me, so I could get lots of work done.

Nevertheless, your office type often reflects your status in the academic pecking system. Presidents and Provosts typically have the nicest digs, while graduate assistants on contract work at the library out of their knapsacks, and mark their territory, with their materials spread out on a big table or nearby chairs.

Contents

Offices are not only places to work and meet students but also spaces to store things. The truth is that many academics are like pack rats. Some find it almost impossible to get into and out of their offices as the doors are partially blocked with academic junk. These are also the professors who lose books, printed articles, physical student assignments, essays, exams, etc. The popular American television show *Hoarders* would have a field day with many of these professors. I suspect that almost every university campus has at least one faculty member whose office is full of stuff that they cannot emotionally let go of. I've heard stories from colleagues, chairs, and administrative staff that they have considered calling the fire department under the pretext that these offices are fire hazards and threaten public safety.

I once took a class from an octogenarian professor whose desk was perpetually buried under a mountain of newspapers. If you dropped in on him during office hours, he would peer around one of the stacks to make eye contact. My adviser, amusingly, kept boxes of IBM punch cards long after the technology had faded into obsolescence. Thankfully, he had the good sense to store them at the top of his gigantic bookshelves that lined the walls. One day when I was an associate professor I got an email from him. He was retiring and cleaning out his office. He had a big cardboard box containing research materials that he had gathered (some four decades prior) that, despite half a dozen cross-country moves, he could not emotionally let go of. He asked me if I had any use for it. Not wishing to be unkind, I unburdened him of this memento. The box sat unopened on my office floor for about five years before I moved offices on campus. I'm relatively confident that it's now at the bottom of some landfill decomposing.

That said, no academic office is complete without an extensive collection of scholarly books, a physical testament to one's knowledge and expertise. A computer is also nonnegotiable. Better yet, having two computers (even better, a desktop and a laptop) or dual monitors adds gravitas, signaling the seriousness of the work you do. And let's not forget a big desk, or perhaps two (hints that you may have people working for you that you must supervise closely), and file cabinets, because who doesn't need a small archive at arm's length? Displaying professional attire, like a well-tailored and pressed dress jacket and contemporary tie or academic regalia, hanging on a coat rack, adds another layer of prestige.

Another phenomenon is if you have a book, it's important to have it prominently displayed. If you have articles, then some professors leave them in a glass case in the hallway or put the front covers on their door. At one point in time, my university took photos of the covers of my books, framed them, and then gave them to me so I could display them on the walls of my office.

How academic offices' aesthetics and functions have evolved

In recent years, driven by the rise of online teaching and pandemic-related shifts, academic offices have become increasingly underutilized or obsolete. Some institutions are even considering repurposing or leasing out these spaces, thereby questioning their relevance in the changing academic landscape. Thus, it's hard not to think that academic offices are beginning to feel more like relics of a bygone era rather than necessities.

Shared offices are becoming more common. And the dreaded "hot desking" trend looms on the horizon. It's increasingly common to hear stories of academics returning to their offices after weeks or months of being absent (i.e., summer break or tenure semester) only to find graduate students or visiting scholars occupying their workspace.

Once, during the last week of my year-long contract as a research assistant, when my contract was about to end at a university, an enterprising office manager moved a handful of excess office furniture into my office to be used as a backup storage space. After all, who was I but a lowly ABD contract research staff?

But what exactly distinguishes the office of an academic criminologist?

Office decor has long reflected professional identity. In today's academic landscape, marked by shrinking spaces and changing modes of university pedagogy, how can criminologists assert their unique presence? Although the above-mentioned standard furniture and decor are common across academic workspaces, certain intangible elements signal disciplinary belonging. These signs and symbols unmistakably mark your office as that of a criminologist and part of the tribe.

Here are a few ideas:

Let's start with what you should not have adorning your office. Unless your kid is an award-winning artist, I would refrain from putting their creative work on the walls. These are better suited to the home refrigerator in your kitchen and not on your office wall. On the other hand, ensure that you have:

Mementos from the field: Showcase police officers' hats or baseball caps with agency insignia or patches, mugs, badges, or memorabilia from criminal justice agencies you've worked for, with, or visited. Extra credit if these items are from international organizations because nothing says "seasoned practitioner" like global bling. Have them lined up in a row and clearly visible. Alternatively, were you ever in the military, National Guard, or reserves? Okay, how about Boy Scouts? If you have legitimate official-looking patches, display them under glass, in a frame, and hang them on the wall. If you don't have anything like that, then the orange safety vest and flashlight you have been given by the assistant dean to be used as the hall monitor in case a fire breaks out might suffice.

Certificates of achievement: Did you attend a special training class with a local criminal justice agency, and they gave you a letter or certificate acknowledging participation? How about when you reviewed a paper for a journal like *Criminology*? If not, did you attend a WordPerfect workshop as a graduate student? Did the organizer give everyone a certificate of completion? Purchase a low-cost glass or plastic frame, insert the document, and affix it to a wall in your office so that it's visible to visitors. Rest assured, no one will be in your office long enough to read these documents closely.

Photos of influence: A framed picture of you shaking hands with a former director of the Department of Justice, Federal Bureau of Investigation, or National Institute of Justice instantly conveys credibility. Perhaps you have one of these lingering in the bottom of your file cabinet drawers, in a cardboard box in your attic or basement; you did not have the heart to throw it out in the last move; it's time to resurrect it. Were you in the military? Do you have pictures that look impressive? If push comes to shove, find something appropriate online with someone of importance shaking another person's hands. That might work.

Subject-relevant books: Having numerous criminology-related books on your shelf is helpful. How do you go about building this collection? If you have not accumulated these tomes via your undergraduate and graduate school education, then acquire them when professors in your department or allied ones clean out their offices. These books are often left in the hallways for local scavengers to pick through. This situation is especially prevalent when these instructors or professors change academic jobs, retire, or die. It's best if they are classic books in the field. If you want a head start, consult the letter in this book, *My Go-To Books in Criminology/Criminal Justice*.

Field-relevant peer-reviewed journals: Be sure to have numerous scholarly journals lined up chronologically on your bookshelves. If you have the space, keep a neat stack of criminology and criminal justice journals on your desk. Bonus points if they are peer-reviewed classics. No one needs to know you read everything online now.

In the end, your office decor is more than just decoration. It's a narrative, a statement, and a little performance art. So, how will you decorate your sacred space?

PART II

Educational and training path/s

Letter 11

WHAT CLASSES SHOULD HIGH SCHOOL STUDENTS WHO WANT TO BECOME CRIMINOLOGY/CRIMINAL JUSTICE PROFESSORS TAKE?

Although I once gave an informal talk about my work to elementary school students at my children's public school, I haven't had the chance to speak with high schoolers specifically interested in academic criminology. That said, although I expect such students exist, I'm not aware of any primary and secondary schools offering criminology/criminal justice-focused classes, apart from general law-related courses.

Truth be told, it does not matter what classes you take during high school if you want to become an academic criminologist. Being a professor of criminology/criminal justice requires more than the coursework you took in high school. Neither the directors of undergraduate nor graduate programs in criminology/criminal justice care about what classes you took at the high school level. Where coursework typically matters is at the doctoral level. If you take graduate-level classes, the hiring committee may look at them, and if you did well in them, they may give legitimacy to your candidacy.

DOI: 10.4324/9781003499145-14

Letter 12

IS EARNING A DEGREE IN CRIMINOLOGY/ CRIMINAL JUSTICE A GOOD STEP IF I WANT TO BE A CRIMINAL PROFILER?

Every academic year, sometimes each semester, I usually have one or more undergraduate students tell me they want to work as a criminal profiler for the Federal Bureau of Investigation (FBI). Influenced by television series such as *CSI* or movies like *The Silence of the Lambs* (neither of which I am a big fan of), they find the depictions of profilers and their work interesting, engaging, and exciting.

Although this particular career aspiration sounds appealing, criminal justice educators should realistically address students' job choices and career expectations. These individuals are often unaware of the necessary coursework, training, and competitive nature of becoming an FBI profiler.

I usually ask students if they know what is required to be a profiler and if they have reviewed relevant job postings. This often results in blank stares or a subdued "no." Unfortunately, this interaction is usually the last I hear about their career aspirations during the semester.

Nevertheless, as the semester progresses (assuming they remain enrolled in the class), these students may look visibly bored or reconsider their desire to become criminal profilers. As they encounter actual criminological research, including empirical studies of crime patterns, policy analysis, and critique of the criminal justice systems, the gap between media fantasy and scholarly reality widens. The career they imagined doesn't align with what criminology/criminal justice actually teaches, because this field, at its best, is a social science, not detective fiction. I rarely ask them in detail about their change of heart. Similar to many of my students who aspire to be police officers or criminal lawyers, at some point during their undergraduate studies, their enthusiasm for this career path dampens.

DOI: 10.4324/9781003499145-15

Nonetheless, one of the most well-known programs for training profilers is offered through the Behavioral Sciences Unit at the FBI Academy in Quantico, VA. Although these courses are primarily designed for law enforcement officers, military personnel, intelligence professionals, and individuals in related fields, one does not need to be an FBI agent to participate. However, candidates must meet specific eligibility criteria and be sponsored by their respective law enforcement agencies to attend. This training attracts participants from across the United States and the world, with classes focused on behavioral science and profiling.

Additionally, there are very few profiler jobs, at least in the manner that students dream of becoming. And in many ways, profiling is unscientific and suffers from confirmation biases. Keep in mind that much of what criminologists teach is only tangentially related to the work of criminal profilers. Taking classes in criminal behavior, criminalistics, and forensics, especially those related to death investigation, might be helpful. Although enrolling in and completing courses in these subjects can be beneficial, not all departments, schools, and colleges of criminology/criminal justice offer these kinds of classes.

There are many different steps students can take to maximize their chances of becoming a profiler with the FBI and opportunities in various industries beyond that agency. Although a degree in criminology or criminal justice is useful, other disciplines, particularly psychology, emphasizing forensic psychology, may be more helpful in becoming a profiler.

As academic criminologists, our role extends beyond conducting important research and imparting accurate information to our students and other audiences. We also break down stereotypes, challenge myths, and provide others with a realistic understanding of crime, criminals, and the criminal justice system. This includes the professionals who respond to crime, the news media, and the victims affected by it. A holistic approach ensures that students are well-prepared for their careers and grasp the complexities of the field they seek to enter.

Suggested reading

Messer, C. M. (2005). *The professionalization of profilers.* Master's Thesis. Oklahoma State University.

Scherer, J. A., & Jarvis, J. P. (2014). Criminal investigative analysis: Practitioner perspectives (Part 2 of 4). *FBI Law Enforcement Bulletin.* Retrieved July 29, 2025. https://leb.fbi.gov/articles/featured-articles/criminal-investigative-analysis-practitioner-perspectives-part-two-of-four

Letter 13

DOES EARNING A PHD IN CRIMINOLOGY/CRIMINAL JUSTICE ENABLE SOMEBODY TO COMMIT THE PERFECT MURDER?[1]

The December 2022 arrest of Washington State University criminology graduate student Bryan Kohberger as the suspected murderer of four University of Idaho students prompted some people, including members of the news media, to ask if earning a degree in criminology or criminal justice motivates someone to commit a crime and/or believe that they can get away with murder/homicide.

Although there is some logic to this question, the short answer is maybe, but not likely.

Why? About four interrelated reasons cast doubt on this kind of thinking.

First, earning a degree in a particular academic field doesn't mean that the recipient of said achievement will use the knowledge they acquired or skills they mastered to engage in deviant or criminal behavior. If this were the case, more pharmacy students would become drug manufacturers and dealers, and computer science students would engage in cybercrime.

Second, every year, many students earn undergraduate and graduate degrees in criminology/criminal justice. Very few of them, however, commit crimes, much less murder. If the pursuit of or earning of a degree in criminology/criminal justice enabled students or graduates to get away with murder, then we would probably see a lot more people fitting this description arrested and charged with homicide or other types of newsworthy crimes, which isn't the case. I would also argue that the average criminology/criminal justice student is more interested in catching bad guys (and women) and assisting victims of crime rather than using this knowledge to "commit the perfect crime."

DOI: 10.4324/9781003499145-16

Third, there are many reasons why people commit murder, and very few criminology/criminal justice students believe that they are smart enough or have the appropriate knowledge or skills to outwit homicide investigators, judges, and juries. I would even speculate that there is an even smaller number of people who think or believe that they can get away with murder because of their knowledge or mastery of forensic science (i.e., the collection and scientific analysis of legal evidence).

Fourth, most individuals who commit a murder are NOT in the process of earning an advanced degree in criminology/criminal justice. They come from other professions and vocations.

Where does this leave us?

Although asking provocative questions about perpetrators' motivations is important and interesting, the public, especially the news media, must move beyond simplistic thinking. They would be better off assuming that there are deeper, complex rationales for why people engage in extreme kinds of human behavior like murder.

Note

1 An earlier version of this letter appeared as "Does Earning a Degree in Criminology/Criminal Justice Help Someone Get Away with Murder?" January 9, 2023. https://jeffreyianross.com/does-earning-a-degree-in-criminology-criminal-justice-help-someone-get-away-with-murder/

Letter 14

WHAT LEVEL OF EDUCATION IS REQUIRED TO BE AN ACADEMIC CRIMINOLOGIST? DOES A PERSON NEED TO EARN A DOCTORATE TO BECOME A CRIMINOLOGIST?

Under normal circumstances, individuals wishing to work as academic criminologists need to have earned a doctorate. In principle, the PhD should be in the field of criminology/criminal justice; however, because criminology/criminal justice is interdisciplinary, it's common for a criminologist to earn a doctorate in a related field such as anthropology, history, political science, psychology, public policy, sociology, or one of several other social sciences. The more important factor is not the specific field of the doctorate but the candidate's research and teaching focus.

That being said, over the past two decades, there has been a proliferation of universities offering doctorates in criminology/criminal justice. This has led to an increasingly protectionist stance, with more departments, schools, and colleges of criminology/criminal justice preferring to hire candidates with doctorates in this specific field and reluctance to employ suitable candidates in the previously mentioned cognate disciplines.

Regardless, if you pursue a doctorate, ensure it's from an accredited institution. And that the accredited body is respected. Although numerous online universities have formed their own accrediting organizations, regional accreditation, such as that granted by the Middle States Commission on Higher Education or similar bodies, is generally considered a mark of institutional credibility. Many unaccredited or low-quality universities will accept students' tuition and provide coursework, but reputable employers, including most accredited universities, may not recognize their degrees. While some practitioners earn doctorates from such institutions, these credentials are often not considered appropriate for academic or professional advancement.

In order to improve the overall the quality of the discipline, the Academy of Criminal Justice Sciences initiated a system where university-level

DOI: 10.4324/9781003499145-17

criminal justice programs could seek certification. However, after about a decade in operation, with only 15 bachelor's and master's level programs having applied for and been granted this status, the program was in 2018 unceremoniously shut down. No doctoral-granting programs ever applied or were evaluated (Worley, 2025).

Taking things one step further, I've only known a few criminologists who either never earned a doctorate or earned it much later in their careers. Such individuals may have completed all the coursework for their PhDs but never finished their dissertations; thus, they did not possess a doctorate. Regardless, the professors I've in mind were highly prolific and well-respected scholars, which may have contributed to their hiring by the academic institutions they worked for. Deep down, these colleagues may have wished to complete their doctorates, but "life got in the way" (i.e., priorities like teaching, advising, administrative responsibilities, family obligations, etc.).

Why is a doctorate necessary, and why is a master's degree insufficient? This has a lot to do with the additional training you receive or are expected to receive at the PhD level. While research productivity is important in most hiring decisions, the majority of academic institutions still require a doctorate, particularly in criminology/criminal justice or a closely related field. The emphasis on doctoral training is also shaped by the structure of the academic labor market itself.

Ultimately, however, with most academic organizations, it's not the possession of a doctorate that matters most, but the quality and amount of research you do.

One last thing: Based on the most recent Association of Doctoral Programs in Criminology & Criminal Justice report (ADPCCJ, 2014),

> 88% of all doctoral graduates want an academic job. In 2014, three-fourths of doctoral graduates were employed in tenure-track academic positions, 13% were employed at federal, state, or local agencies as an agency head or researcher, and less than 1% were employed through private research firms. (Alarid, 2016)

Suggested reading

Alarid, L.F. (2016). How to Secure your First Academic Job Out of Graduate School. *Journal of Criminal Justice Education*, 27(2), 160–174.

Association of Doctoral Programs in Criminology and Criminal Justice. (2014). *2014 Survey report.* http://www.adpccj.com

Carlan, P. E., Lewis, J. A., & Dial, K. C. (2009). Faculty diversity and program standing in criminology and criminal justice: Findings for 31 doctoral programs in 2008. *Journal of Criminal Justice Education*, *20*(3), 249–271.

Worley, R. M. (2025). *Of beignets, boardrooms, and bureaucracy: The untold story of the demise of ACJS certification* [Unpublished manuscript]. ResearchGate. Retrieved July 31, 2025, https://www.researchgate.net/publication/391704765_Of_Beignets_Boardrooms_and_Bureaucracy_The_Untold_Story_of_the_Demise_of_ACJS_Certification#fullTextFileContent

Letter 15

I HAVE A LAW DEGREE. WHAT ARE MY CHANCES OF BEING HIRED AS A CRIMINOLOGIST FOR A DEPARTMENT, SCHOOL, OR COLLEGE OF CRIMINOLOGY/CRIMINAL JUSTICE?

Congratulations on graduating from law school! It's a significant achievement that reflects your dedication, tenacity, and hard work. If you've gained practical experience in criminal law, whether in a prosecutor's office, with a defense attorney, or another setting, that background can be invaluable not just in legal practice but in policy work and academic settings. If you've considered teaching in a criminology or criminal justice program, that could be another rewarding avenue to explore.

Unquestionably, departments of criminology and criminal justice employ individuals with JDs or other legal training to teach classes in criminal law, evidence, and sentencing. However, such roles are typically part-time or adjunct positions. Rarely are people with only a Juris Doctorate (JD) hired for full-time jobs, particularly tenure-track ones in these departments, and there are logical reasons why.

Although scholars with Juris Doctorates (JDs) (e.g., Herman Goldstein, Michael Tonry, and Frank Zimring), or Doctorates in Law (e.g., Norval Morris) have made significant contributions to criminology and criminal justice, they have typically held faculty positions in law schools, public policy programs, or interdisciplinary research institutes rather than criminology or criminal justice departments. Generally, an earned JD alone is insufficient for tenure-track employment in criminology, unless accompanied by additional credentials, such as a PhD in a relevant field. Individuals with JDs may be hired part-time to teach law-related courses, but full-time faculty positions in criminology generally require expertise in criminological theory and research methods, which are not the primary focus of legal education.

DOI: 10.4324/9781003499145-18

Predictably, the issue of hiring JDs for tenure-track jobs has been hotly debated in criminology and criminal justice circles, leading to numerous articles in scholarly journals and academic criminal justice newsletters (e.g., *ACJS Today*).

Why are most departments of criminology reluctant to hire JDs full-time? There are countless reasons. This isn't simply a protectionist move. According to Madden and Hartley (2011),

> the education of the JD isn't sufficient to provide a base for the primary duties of faculty: teaching and research. JDs are trained to be lawyers, to write briefs and argue intrinsic points of Law (codified and case), not to conduct social science research. (pp. 440–441)

Put another way, the knowledge and training one receives to become a lawyer is highly specialized. Although you may know all the tricks of the trade in lawyering, including writing legal briefs, you probably don't have the foggiest idea about criminological theory, research methods, and the vast scholarship on the various branches of criminal justice.

The subject matter of criminology/criminal justice is much broader than law, and criminal law in particular, and thus, the departments wish to hire individuals with a relatively comprehensive view of the discipline. Madden and Hartley (2011) add that,

> JDs are limited in the number of courses they can teach within a criminological curriculum. Unlike a PhD, who should be well versed in a variety of topics within the field (both content areas, such as policing or criminological theory, and research methods/statistics), JDs have only been educated in areas of the law. (pp. 440–441)

That said, it's not impossible for someone with a JD to be hired as a tenure-track criminologist. You can tip the balance in your favor by doing a handful of things. In addition to teaching the aforementioned classes in departments of criminology/criminal justice, you can demonstrate a pattern of consistent scholarship in criminology/criminal justice journals. This may begin with teaming up with one or more appropriate criminologists who will mentor you in this process.

Concurrently, you might consider earning a master's degree (or a PhD) in criminology/criminal justice from a respected university. In fact, candidates with JDs from top institutions of higher learning and a PhD from a respected criminology/criminal justice program are often the most desirable job candidates. But you must carefully weigh the possible costs and benefits of these decisions. In other words, it's essential to ask yourself if the added investment of time and money will be worth the benefit.

Suggested reading

Hemmens, C. (2008). Waist deep in the big muddy: The JD/PhD debate in criminal justice education. *Journal of Criminal Justice Education*, *19*(1), 19–29.

Hemmens, C. (2015). We [should] take care of our own: The role of law and lawyers in criminal justice and criminology programs. *Justice Quarterly*, *32*(5), 749–767.

Madden, S., & Hartley, R. D. (2011). Lawyers practicing medicine: Criminal justice, criminology, sociology, and differential curricula. *Journal of Criminal Justice Education*, *22*(3), 440–465.

Letter 16

SHOULD I EARN A PHD IN CRIMINOLOGY/CRIMINAL JUSTICE OR AN ALLIED FIELD?[1]

Somewhere in the back of your mind, a voice insists: Earn a PhD in criminology/criminal justice. For many students, this impulse is shaped less by a clear understanding of what doctoral training involves, but because their impressions come from than by cultural imagery of academia and their experiences as undergraduates.

Perhaps you like to binge on late-night TV shows featuring handsome, charismatic police officers and drop-dead gorgeous and brilliant detectives solving complex or horrendous crimes. Alternatively, maybe your passion for higher learning was ignited during your undergraduate years when entertaining, engaging, or supportive criminology professors inspired you to explore the intricacies of crime and the criminal justice system more deeply. And to you, this means that the only viable answer is to earn a PhD in criminology/criminal justice.

Before applying to doctoral programs in criminology or criminal justice, consider completing a master's program first. This can provide valuable preparation, particularly for students who are unsure about committing to a PhD right away. In the United States, there are more master's programs than PhD programs in these fields, and for good reason. Master's programs offer foundational training in research and theory, which can enhance your readiness for doctoral study. Additionally, some universities offer interdisciplinary doctoral programs, such as a doctorate in public policy, that accept students from related master's programs.

Although some PhD programs admit students directly with a bachelor's degree, completing a master's first can help clarify your research interests and strengthen your academic foundation. Additionally, many master's programs do not require a thesis, which may be a factor to consider depending on your goals.

DOI: 10.4324/9781003499145-19

However, suppose you're convinced you want to earn a doctorate (or even a master's), it's important to ask yourself some key questions. To help you navigate this decision, here are several interrelated ones, ranked in order of importance.

1. What are your passions, strong interests, etc.?

To begin with, reflect on what motivates you the most. Also, it might be a good time to think clearly about the differences among passions, strong interests, etc. (Skip now to the last letter in this book if this specific discussion interests you, and return to this letter when completed.)

2. Can you achieve your career goals without a PhD in criminology/criminal justice?

This may be a good time to reexamine the specific career path you aspire to and consider whether a PhD is necessary for your goals. Many people think that the only way to achieve ambitious and meaningful goals is through more formal education, when they would be better served by skill development, exposure, experience, volunteering, or working in a relevant setting.

3. Do you know the costs and benefits of earning a PhD versus other career choices?

A PhD isn't for everyone. You will likely spend many hours in the library reading books and articles that often do not make sense to you. They may also deal with topics, that you believe to be unnecessarily obscure. Alternatively, or concurrently, you might invest lots of time in the field talking with, interviewing, and/or observing people and situations that deep down are hostile to your presence. You will most likely be collecting and analyzing data, which can be ridiculously tedious and mind-numbing. Many of your fellow graduate students and professors may not be generous with their time and expertise. Unlike many skilled trades (e.g., plumber, electrician, etc.) and professions (e.g., doctor, lawyer, etc.) that people train for, there are fewer job openings upon completion, and it is unclear that your investment will pay off with a good-paying career and salary. Moreover, you may have to work in a place you do not want to live in, and for a considerable period of time.

4. Should you commit to a PhD in criminology/criminal justice, or is it better to explore an allied cognate field, like history, political science, public policy, or sociology?

According to Geis, who, along with Dodge, edited *The Lessons of Criminology* (2002), a book of short autobiographies written by well-known criminologists, indicated that "several of the writers endorse immersion in another not notably close subject area in addition to criminology and criminal justice to provide a more cosmopolitan insight into their major criminological concerns" (p. xii). This advice should be taken into consideration. This approach may open up alternative job and research possibilities for you.

5. Which allied discipline/s also align best with your interests?

Is it possible to earn a PhD in sociology, political science, or public policy while researching criminological topics? And is a doctorate in criminology or criminal justice the best option, or can similar goals be achieved in an allied field? The answer depends on multiple factors, including disciplinary norms, faculty expertise, and career aspirations.

With some creativity and the support of a receptive mentor and committee, students in various disciplines can frame their research in ways that engage both their home field and criminology/criminal justice. For example, a history PhD student interested in prisons would naturally engage with corrections scholarship. Similarly, a political science PhD focused on policing could incorporate criminological theories while maintaining alignment with political science debates.

However, disciplinary expectations and job market considerations should not be overlooked. Some mentors and committees may encourage interdisciplinary work, while others expect strict adherence to field-specific frameworks.

6. Will earning a PhD in criminology/criminal justice make you more marketable than securing a PhD in another field?

Research the current job market for a recently graduated PhD in criminology/criminal justice, and try to get a handle on the supply and demand for people with this qualification compared to individuals who have earned doctorates in other disciplines. And keep in mind that the supply and demand for people with particular PhDs varies over time. For instance, this year, there may be more job openings for individuals with earned doctorates in one type of social science; next year, it's for another. This year, criminologists with expertise in policing may be in high demand, and the following hiring season it's for people who know something about juvenile justice.

7. Should you start with a master's degree before taking the plunge with a PhD?

Although your ego might be stoked by earning a PhD, if you don't already have a master's degree in criminology/criminal justice, you might want to start by earning this type of degree first before considering moving on to the PhD. Treat the master's degree process (especially one that requires a thesis) like an experiment. It's a close approximation of what you might expect during a PhD program.

8. Can you secure funding to earn a doctorate in criminology or criminal justice, or is it easier to get financing in another field?

Assuming that you're not independently wealthy, explore scholarship opportunities, assistantships, and grants available in both criminology/criminal justice versus cognate fields. Often, funding is directly related to the research projects that professors in the target departments to which you're applying have. For example, if you want funding and a professor has a gun violence research study, assume that you will be working closely with that professor on this topic and that they will have money in their research grant to support your tuition.

9. Should you pursue your PhD in a department where the curriculum and professors equally emphasize criminology and criminal justice?

Although criminology and criminal justice are related, they are not the same field. And not all PhD programs are equivalent. They employ instructors, professors, and staff with subdisciplinary expertise, strengths, and weaknesses. Some emphasize research, while others focus on teaching, and others strike a balance. Some faculty members are knowledgeable about the latest research, while others are not well-versed in the current debates. It's important to check this out before enrolling; otherwise, you may be surprised or disappointed with your chosen instructors, mentors, and program.

10. Is there a well-respected criminologist (who can also act as your mentor) with whom you would like to work in a PhD program in criminology or criminal justice?

In many respects, more significant than the subject matter of the discipline in which you want to earn a PhD are the potential advisors (and mentors) who align with your research interests and career aspirations. It helps if there are one or more well-known scholars in the department you want to apply to whose specialization aligns with yours, who are easy to work with, and who can appropriately mentor you. If that magic person does not exist, then there are numerous fallback strategies you can pursue.

11. Is there a respected PhD program in criminology/criminal justice close to where you live?

When evaluating a program, consider not just its quality but its geographic location too. If you have a partner, family, children, or aging parents, consider whether relocation would significantly disrupt your lifestyle, loved ones, and social connections. Is there a way to strike a balance by choosing a more convenient yet reputable option? Explore whether the program offers face-to-face only or online courses, how many, and whether they are required or elective. Finally, reflect on your learning preferences: Do you thrive in face-to-face settings, or are you comfortable with online instruction?

12. Should you work on your PhD full-time or part-time? Are there one or more respected PhD programs in criminology/criminal justice that will allow you to do the work part-time?

Although pursuing your PhD part-time may be appealing, it's also necessary to realize that few programs operate up this way. Many part-time programs are not as rigorous as the ones that demand full-time enrollment. Alternatively, if you attend part-time, many professors and instructional staff do not take you as seriously as you may want them to. It is also much more challenging to secure funding if you only attend part-time.

13. Is it helpful to speak to a qualified career counselor, in addition to the admissions director at the prospective PhD program you want to enter?

If you find it difficult to decide which program to enroll in, then it might be useful to consult an appropriate and qualified career advisor who can provide insights into the job market and the hiring trends relevant to the field/subject matter you want to pursue. They may also know better than you what kinds of formal education and training you need to enter said profession. Sometimes, the school where you earned your bachelor's degree (or master's degree) may offer alumni free career counseling services. And that would be a good place to start.

Next steps

All in all, it's important to do one's due diligence by conducting as much research as possible. This involves not simply consulting the websites of prospective PhD programs, but talking to instructors and current and past graduate students enrolled in PhD programs in criminology/criminal justice (and allied fields). This process should enable you to learn about and hopefully better understand their experiences and the career paths they are considering. Attending one or more criminology/criminal justice conferences and interacting with the attendees is also be advisable.

In conclusion, deciding whether to pursue a PhD in criminology/criminal justice or an allied field is a significant decision. You want to take a calculated risk, have a Plan B if the graduate program doesn't work out for you, and consider pivoting into something else that interests you, adequately pays the bills, gives you a modicum of fulfillment, and doesn't force you into perpetual student loan debt. This may include a different subject to do your PhD in, or a different career to explore.

In many respects, the concerns of graduate students in criminology/criminal justice are no different from those in all other fields. The central question is whether a job will be waiting for them when they complete their PhD. In short, the basic question is whether all the effort is worth it.

In other words, there is no one-size-fits-all answer, and your decision should ultimately reflect your aspirations and life circumstances.

Note

1 An earlier version of this letter appeared as "Should You Earn a PhD in Criminology/Criminal Justice or an Allied Field?" October 21, 2023. https://jeffreyianross.com/should-you-earn-a-phd-in-criminology-criminal-justice-or-an-allied-field/

Suggested reading

Bufkin. (2004). Criminology/criminal justice master's programs in the United States: Searching for commonalities, *Journal of Criminal Justice Education*, *15*(2), 239–262.

Enriquez, R. (2008). Criminal justice faculty credentials: A response to Drs. Hemmens and Hunter. *Journal of Criminal Justice Education*, *19*(2), 205–212.

Hunter, R. (2008). Why we need certification standards in criminal justice education and what the impacts will be: A response to the concerns of JDs. *Journal of Criminal Justice Education*, *19*(2), 193–204.

Morreale, S. A., & McCabe, J. E. (2014). Assessing hiring preferences and discipline orientation of criminal justice programs. *Journal of International Criminal Justice Research*, *2*(1), 1–18.

Letter 17

WHAT IS THE BEST PHD PROGRAM FOR EARNING A GRADUATE DEGREE IN CRIMINOLOGY AND CRIMINAL JUSTICE?

Every year, the *U.S. News & World Report* ranks the top PhD-granting departments, schools, and colleges in criminology and criminal justice in the United States. And each time, the same institutions get listed in the top ten (e.g., University of California, Irvine; University of Pennsylvania; University of Florida; University of Maryland, College Park; University of Cincinnati; Michigan State University; John Jay College of Criminal Justice (CUNY); Florida State University; University of Texas at Dallas; and Northeastern University). Meanwhile, other schools, such as Rutgers, Sam Houston, and American University, cycle on and off the top ten list.

And if you want to really get into the weeds, you can consult successive issues of the *Journal of Criminal Justice Education* and read articles that rank the departments on different measures. Over the years and periodically, scholars like to compare which departments are the most productive, whose members are most cited, etc.

One thing that you should immediately notice is that, except for the University of Pennsylvania, none of the Ivy League universities, like Columbia, Princeton, Yale, etc., have departments of criminology. While each of the Ivys has one or more criminologists, they typically work in departments of sociology, schools of public policy, or law schools.

Unquestionably, students considering earning a master's or PhD at these schools can get a decent education. However, despite the rankings, there are many subtle but important factors beyond the rankings that individuals considering graduate school should consider. This includes: Is the department more or less practitioner or research-oriented? What is their success rate in placing students in jobs in criminal justice agencies, research consulting

DOI: 10.4324/9781003499145-20

firms, and universities? Are the faculty disproportionately young or old? Is there diversity among the faculty and student body regarding subject matter specialization, methodological preferences, age, race/ethnicity, gender, etc.?

Prospective students should also be aware of noncareer-related things like the organizational culture of the programs, departments, schools, colleges, and universities. Don't simply rely on the information you find on their website or gleaned via a handful of phone calls or emails to the graduate director. That being said, if you're asking questions about these issues, expect that much of the evidence produced will be descriptive and anecdotal. And if you enroll in the program without attempting to answer these questions, you may be in for some significant culture shock, and your expectations may be dashed.

As a candidate, know what you want from these schools and work settings. Unfortunately, many aspiring criminologists entering graduate school have unrealistic expectations about what grad programs, professors, academia, and student life are like. And there are different norms and realities concerning these elements among departments, even on the same campus.

Thus, it's wise to conduct some personal qualitative (e.g., ethnographic and observational) research. If possible, visit these programs in person while classes are in session. At the very least, take the formal university tour and speak with the graduate director, instructors, professors, prospective mentors, and graduate students in criminology and criminal justice programs.

Before your visit, contact the department's director of graduate studies. This preliminary work should also include connecting with a diverse group of graduate students (at different stages of their education), instructors, professors (at different ranks), and staff, not just those who happen to be on campus that day. Remember that individuals you meet during a visit may present the program in its best light or may have stuck around to share their personal beef and warn you off. If you're unable to meet key people in person, consider following up via phone or video call (e.g., Zoom, FaceTime, etc.).

In some departments, grad students go out drinking with their professors, instructors, and staff. In others, they may have rotating potlucks at each other's residences, and then again, in different situations, students may never see each other the entire semester outside of class. Which type of program do you prefer? That is why campus visits are often helpful when classes are held (not during exam week). After all, just like any skilled scholar, you're practicing the collection and interpretation of data.

Also, just because *U.S. News & World Report* ranks American schools should not prevent you from considering excellent criminology and criminal justice doctoral programs in other countries, such as Canada, the United Kingdom, Australia, and Europe.

If that is the case, you should consult three sources: QS World University Rankings, the Shanghai Global Ranking of Academic Subjects, and the Times Higher Education Ranking. Remember, however, that none of these specifically rank criminology departments, but they will rank the broader social sciences and law and legal studies programs.

There are definitely advantages and disadvantages to studying overseas in terms of models of instruction, research foci, cost, and the networks you will be tapping into.

Again, remember that the criteria you deem essential are the most necessary in your choice for a particular school. Also, keep in mind that regardless of where you choose to earn your master's and doctorate, and your subject specialization, as you progress through a post-bachelor's degree, the possibility that your preferences may change regarding what you think is important.

Suggested reading

Schildkraut, J., & Stafford, M. C. (2015). Researching professionals or professional researchers? A comparison of professional doctorate and PhD programs in criminology & criminal justice. *American Journal of Criminal Justice*, *40*(1), 183–198.

Letter 18

WHERE CAN GRADUATE STUDENTS IN THE FIELD OF CRIMINOLOGY/ CRIMINAL JUSTICE LOOK FOR FUNDING FOR THEIR EDUCATION?

Regardless of the discipline, attending graduate school, paying for living expenses, going to conferences, and conducting master's and doctoral-level research can be expensive. A frequent question is: How can graduate students pay for all these things? In general, there are traditional sources like parents, spouses, loved ones, personal savings, and student grants and loans, sometimes from the federal government or from the university where they will be taking classes.

Students wishing to apply for funding are encouraged to check with the individual departments, especially the graduate advisors. They may know what grants and scholarships are available. If one exists, students should also check with the College of Graduate Studies, which coordinates lots of important things for graduate students.

There may also be so-called hidden (i.e., less well-known) funding sources (often tied to a specific activity) for criminology/criminal justice students.

Regarding tuition, many departments often offer one or more tuition-free grants to incoming master's or doctoral students. This money may be based on specific criteria, such as grades, underrepresented minorities, women, etc. If not at the department level, these grants may be available through the dean's or provost's offices. Sometimes, the graduate school, if one exists at the institution you want to study at, offers a limited number of scholarships and fellowships. Investigating these on your own early in the application process is helpful.

If you work for a criminal justice agency, it may pay full or part tuition for bachelor's, master's, and doctoral-level instruction. Some of these entities predictably offer better financial support than others. If you're a

DOI: 10.4324/9781003499145-21

union member, the organization may also allocate funds to support workers attending graduate school or conferences as part of its mission.

Concerning the last option, you might start by asking your supervisor or department for funding for travel to the annual meetings of the criminology/criminal justice learned society of your choice. Sometimes, if you're working with a professor on a scholarly paper, and that research is funded, and they are attending the annual meeting, the grant budget may include funding to take you along. If no money is available, you should start making your way up the chain of command at the university you attend (i.e., dean's office, provost's office, etc.).

Also, the major learned criminology/criminal justice organizations (ASC, ACJS, etc.) and their divisions (e.g., Division of Convict Criminology) often have some funding to subsidize a handful of grad students to attend their meetings to present papers. Still, this support rarely covers all costs.

Letter 19

ARE SOME PUBLICATION OUTLETS MORE FRIENDLY FOR GRADUATE STUDENTS IN CRIMINOLOGY/CRIMINAL JUSTICE?

There are numerous publication outlets for criminologists, as well as for those aspiring to enter the field. But, where and how you publish your work depends on several factors.

Some types of research and writing are easier to publish in certain venues than others. Outlets with lower submission barriers include division newsletters of learned associations (e.g., ASC, ACJS), followed by the newsletter of the larger organization, blogs, book reviews, and similar formats.

Many encyclopedia editors accept submissions from graduate students. Sometimes, students discover these opportunities and ask their Ph.D. advisors whether they should attempt to publish solo or coauthor. Other times, advisors invite students to collaborate on these entries. Coauthoring is an essential pedagogical model in graduate education, with faculty mentors guiding students through the publishing process. Ideally, publishing with your advisor provides valuable experience as they are in a position to help navigate the nuances of academic publishing.

A similar dynamic occurs with handbook chapters, which often feature multiple authors. In many cases, a graduate student's role is relatively minor, such as tracking down missing references, cleaning them up (e.g., finding omitted dates of publications, the volumes or issues they appeared in, or the pages), ensuring proper formatting, and their name appears last in the author list.

In some cases, the bar for acceptance may be lower for special issues of academic journals, particularly when editors need broad coverage. Some special issue editors take a more hands-on approach, offering constructive feedback to authors and pointing out key research or citations a scholar may

DOI: 10.4324/9781003499145-22

have overlooked. However, special issues in top-tier journals can still be highly selective with respect to the material that ends up being published.

While these types of outlets can be appealing due to their relatively quick turnaround times, they should be seen as stepping stones rather than the foundation of an academic career. In other words, they can help build your CV but should not define your scholarly identity.

Over time, you should aim to publish your research in increasingly prestigious venues. Generally, the more selective a publication outlet is, the more valuable it is to your academic career.

Suggested reading

Hoover, K. B., & Lucas, K. T. (2023). Mentoring graduate students: A study on academic rejection, the pressure to publish, and career paths. *Journal of Criminal Justice Education*, *35*(1), 195–217.

Letter 20

SHOULD CRIMINOLOGISTS BE SKEPTICAL OF PEOPLE WHO SEEM TO HAVE ALL THE ANSWERS TO CRIME, CRIME CONTROL, AND CRIMINAL JUSTICE REFORM?

Yes. Criminologists should be skeptical of anyone (i.e., politicians, community leaders, activists, or even fellow scholars) who claim to have all the answers about crime, crime control, or criminal justice reform. No one holds a monopoly on truth in this field, and overconfidence is often a red flag. Even a broken clock is right twice a day, and if it's digital, maybe only once. The point is: Being occasionally correct doesn't make someone reliably informed.

Crime and criminal justice are not just empirical matters; they are deeply political. Policies, practices, and laws are shaped by values, interests, ideologies, and power, not just by evidence. People in positions of authority or with large public platforms are often mistaken for experts, but visibility does not guarantee insight. Policymakers especially are frequently driven by electoral incentives and may lack the substantive knowledge required for meaningful reform.

For these reasons, criminologists must approach all claims critically. Everyone brings biases to the table. Those perspectives must be examined thoughtfully, and claims, no matter their source, should be tested against rigorous empirical evidence. Our responsibility is not to offer simple answers but to ask better questions, expose flawed reasoning, and bring clarity to complex issues.

DOI: 10.4324/9781003499145-23

Letter 21

WHAT ARE MY FAVORITE BOOKS IN THE FIELD OF CRIMINOLOGY/CRIMINAL JUSTICE?

Although tempted to only list the books I authored, coauthored, edited, or coedited, I will refrain from taking this approach. To begin with, I encourage all students, criminal justice practitioners, instructors, and scholars to read widely. In other words, don't just read scholarly articles, chapters, and books in the discipline of criminology/criminal justice, but expose yourself to materials in the cognate fields (e.g., anthropology, history, political science, sociology, etc.). I also recommend reading a respected newspaper (e.g., *The New York Times*) and blog posts on a regular basis. Moreover, listening to podcasts and music, and watching movies expands your base of knowledge. These cultural artifacts may not be helpful on an informational basis. But, they can be sources of inspiration for projects, including ones that involve research and provide content that acts as bridges to make connections with your students, colleagues, and perhaps your research subjects.

Now, you're probably saying there are only so many hours in a day to do all this. And you're right. That's why you need to be strategic about what you expose your eyes, ears, and brain to.

Nonetheless, there are probably two basic questions to be answered here: What do others consider classic books, and what do I believe are the most helpful? Every discipline has a canon, and criminology and criminal justice are no different. These articles, chapters, and books are often reflected on reading lists in graduate criminology and criminal justice programs. If you're curious, do a Google search to discover what they are.

Answering what the most influential books for me in the field are, however, is a tricky question. Moreover, there is a difference between what I think have been the most influential books for me and which ones you would

DOI: 10.4324/9781003499145-24

most benefit from reading. Also, remember that when I say reading, I am not just saying read it and check the box; I am talking about understanding the argument and the evidence analyzed at a deeper level.

Also, I am more inclined to recommend books in subspecializations in criminology/criminal justice (e.g., policing, corrections, etc.). For example, I would generally recommend Elijah Anderson's Code *of the Street: Decency, Violence, and the Moral Life of the Inner City*, an ethnography about how informal social rules govern behavior in disadvantaged urban communities and influence crime patterns, but this is a very niche book in the discipline of criminology/criminal justice.

I suspect some of my recommended books would appear in reading lists that graduate students might encounter when studying for their comprehensive exams If you don't have time to read them, at least be familiar with their basic argument/s. Nevertheless, several criminology/criminal justice books have turned the dial for me. I've ranked them from least to most important. These include:

1. *When Crime Waves*, by Vincent Sacco (2005), examines how crime waves are constructed socially and politically, offering insights into the relationship between media, public perception, and criminal justice policy.
2. *Shared Beginnings, Divergent Lives: Delinquent Boys to Age 70*, by John H. Laub and Robert J. Sampson (2003), presents the findings of a longitudinal study that follows juvenile delinquents throughout their lives, providing important insights into criminal persistence and desistance.
3. *The Criminological Imagination*, by Jock Young (2011). Building on C. Wright Mills's classic book, *The Sociological Imagination (1958)*, Young argues that too much of current criminological study is based on statistics. This approach obscures essential nuances in interactions and explanations.
4. Stanley Cohen's *Against Criminology* (1988) is a series of essays that critiques the discipline as overly constrained by its institutional ties and preoccupation with crime control. Cohen argues that criminology often reinforces the systems it claims to study critically. Instead, Cohen advocates for a more reflective and interdisciplinary approach, emphasizing the importance of challenging dominant narratives and exploring broader social, cultural, and political contexts of crime and deviance.
5. *Punishment and Social Structure*, by Georg Rusche and Otto Kirchheimer (1939), links economic conditions to changes in penal policy. This century old book is foundational for understanding penal systems in their social contexts.

6. *Invisible Women: Gender, Crime, and Justice*, by Meda Chesney-Lind and Lisa Pasko (2004), examines how the justice system perpetuates gender inequality, particularly in treating female perpetrators and victims.
7. Although numerous excellent books do a good job of explaining criminological theory, one of the most helpful is *Theoretical Criminology* by George Vold, Thomas J. Bernard, and Jeffrey B. Snipes (1958/1997). These authors provide a comprehensive overview of criminological theories, bridging classical, positivist, and contemporary schools of thought.
8. *The Culture of Control: Crime and Social Order in Contemporary Society*, by David Garland (2001), is worth reading. This book analyzes shifts in crime control strategies in late modernity, focusing on punitive policies and the cultural roots of penal change.
9. *Cultural Criminology: An Invitation*, by Jeff Ferrell, Keith J. Hayward, and Jock Young (2008), builds upon the work that the authors and others have done in this exciting subfield of critical criminology.
10. Jeffrey Reiman and Paul Leighton's *The Rich Get Richer and the Poor Get Prison: Ideology, Class, and Criminal Justice* (1979/2023) analyzes the American criminal justice system and examines how social class influences justice outcomes.
11. *Seductions of Crime: Moral and Sensual Attractions of Delinquency*, by Jack Katz (1988), explores the emotional and sensory experiences that drive individuals to commit crimes. It focuses on how perpetrators find momentary thrills, moral justifications, or transcendence in their actions. Katz emphasizes the importance of understanding these situational and subjective dynamics rather than solely focusing on structural or dispositional explanations for criminal behavior.

It's not necessary to drop everything you are doing and start reading these books. Instead try to tackle them over an identifiable period (e.g., one year), or commit to reading one of these classics before submitting each new paper you have written for peer review. Over time, you will gain additional foundational knowledge and better contextualize the scholarship that you engage in and impart on your students. If you read one or more of these books in graduate school, then it may also be worthwhile to reread them. Happy reading.

Letter 22

HOW CAN I DEEPEN MY KNOWLEDGE OF CRIMINOLOGY/CRIMINAL JUSTICE?

Short of working as a criminal justice practitioner, reading as much as possible in the field, and conducting research to become a more knowledgeable and well-rounded criminologist, take advantage of opportunities to observe or experience selected aspects of the criminal justice system. This includes participating in ride-alongs with law enforcement officers, tours of correctional facilities, and visits to the coroner's office and courtrooms to observe criminal proceedings.

This activity can begin when you are an undergraduate student and continue through your master's and doctoral studies. Doing this when you're an adjunct or even a junior tenure-track professor is also advisable if you were never able to fit this activity in before this point in your career. Sometimes these extracurricular activities are enabled when the criminology/criminal justice student association in your department organizes these kinds of activities, and you act as a chaperone or faculty advisor. Additionally, similar opportunities are available at some of the ASC, ACJS, and regional criminology/criminal justice conferences.

It's also valuable to explore firsthand how criminal justice institutions vary across different levels of government—city, county, state, and federal. Within the United States, you should consider going on ride-alongs with both county and city police to observe the differences in their operations. Comparing motorized patrols with foot patrols can also offer important insights. Additionally, spending time in the field over 24 hours can be instructive. For instance, a night in a dispatch center can be especially helpful, as it allows you to see how decisions are made about which calls for service receive immediate police response and of what magnitude. This kind

DOI: 10.4324/9781003499145-25

of activity can be repeated with different branches of the criminal justice system. Inside the United States, for example, you might visit a correctional facility in a northern city or county, or, if the opportunity arises, one in the South.

There are also clear advantages to observing how criminal justice agencies operate outside the United States. Sometimes the best ideas for criminal justice reform are to be found in other countries, and you may be in an ideal position to bring these ideas back to a criminal justice agency that you have strong ties to in the United States or elsewhere.

Some of the benefits of these experiences include being able to reflect on these experiences in your pedagogy and/or your research.

Overall, these firsthand experiences may cut down on imposter syndrome, which you may suffer from. It's good to observe what's going on and make mental or physical notes. In addition to providing a general description of what occurs, to whom, and why, try to look at how and why these settings differ. How does this compare to your research or the textbook you have assigned to your students?

Also keep in mind that, there is also the phenomenon of diminishing returns. Thus you may want to ask yourself how much value is added to each successive ride-along or correctional facility visit. After your fifth jail visit in the United States, you're unlikely to encounter much additional diversity. Since over time, the experience and the institutions are pretty much the same; a jail is a jail is a jail. Also, as an observer, keep in mind that many of the people you interact with will often be on their best behavior, and you will rarely see parts of a correctional facility that the administrators believe may reflect negatively on the entire institution.

There will always be cost-benefit calculations. More specifically, ask yourself what you hope to gain by visiting criminal justice agencies, and what expense you may incur. Is that at the expense of not spending quality time with your partner, family, and loved ones? Only you can make this decision.

Suggested reading

Piché, J., & Walby, K. (2010). Problematizing carceral tours. *The British Journal of Criminology*, *50*(3), 570–581.

PART III

Job prospects and career trajectories in the academy and beyond

Letter 23

WILL EARNING A PHD IN CRIMINOLOGY ASSIST ME IN BECOMING A CRIME FICTION WRITER?

Maybe you've dreamed of being the next Agatha Christie, James Elroy, or another famous crime fiction writer.

Although a few criminologists made this transition, more realistically, they do this activity on the side. Some, quietly frustrated by the limited financial rewards and public recognition that come with writing academic or textbook material, imagine a literary reinvention. If they pivot to crime fiction, they think, maybe they'll get rich, or at least win the kind of acclaim that writing peer-reviewed articles rarely provides.

Seduced by the illusion of transferable skills, and often unaware of the Dunning-Kruger effect[1] where limited experience breeds overconfidence, some criminologists ask themselves: How hard could it be to write crime fiction? After all, they know a great deal about crime, criminals, and the criminal justice system. Surely that counts for something.

And yes, it does. But knowing how to conduct scholarly research or correct for heteroskedasticity does not mean you know how to plot a compelling narrative, develop complex characters, or build tension across 300 or so pages. Most criminal justice or criminology programs don't offer classes or workshops on dialogue, pacing, or narrative arc.

The desire to switch lanes is understandable. But the assumption that expertise in criminology/criminal justice naturally confers storytelling ability is a leap built on wishful thinking, and often a lack of mentorship. There's a wide gap between understanding the criminal justice system and writing a gripping novel that keeps readers turning pages and buying books.

A more realistic model is for aspiring or established fiction writers to immerse themselves in criminology and criminal justice. Read a handful of

DOI: 10.4324/9781003499145-27

foundational texts. Enroll in a few courses. Interview criminal justice professionals, victims, and even perpetrators of crime. Build a base of knowledge that can enrich your fiction with authenticity.

Interestingly, it's often former law enforcement officers, detectives, or criminal justice agency administrators, not academics, who make the most convincing crime novelists. They draw from years of practical, on-the-job, and in-the-field experience to craft their stories around.

For those criminologists who feel compelled to write crime fiction, wary of the academic judgment or professional jealousy such a move might provoke, publish under a pseudonym. Others try to balance both worlds, producing scholarly work by day, fiction by night.

Many criminologists talk about becoming crime novelists. But only a few take the risk, and fewer still do it well.

Note

1 A cognitive bias where people with low ability or knowledge in a specific area tend to overestimate their competence. Essentially, individuals with lower skill levels may not realize how unskilled they are, leading them to overestimate their abilities.

Letter 24

WILL EARNING A PHD IN CRIMINOLOGY OR CRIMINAL JUSTICE HELP ME GET HIRED AS A CRIMINOLOGIST FOR A CRIMINAL JUSTICE AGENCY OR A RESEARCH CONSULTING ORGANIZATION?

Suppose you want to conduct or manage research for a local, state, or federal criminal justice agency (e.g., National Institute of Justice, The Home Office, etc.) or research consulting organization (e.g., Vera Institute, Urban Institute, Police Foundation, etc.). In that case, you generally need a minimum of a bachelor's degree. But if you want more responsibility, a higher salary, and to be more competitive, a master's degree is usually required. And, depending on a handful of circumstances (such as becoming a study director), a doctorate is typically needed.

In many respects, the requirements for these government and private-sector jobs vary depending on the criminal justice agency, research consultancy, or think tank, as well as its location and hiring criteria. Much of this is related to supply and demand issues. In the United States, many of the research consulting organizations that focus on matters of criminal justice are located in the Washington, DC, area. Pejoratively referred to as Beltway Bandits, they require their research staff to respond to Requests for Proposals issued by government agencies by writing grant applications and, if awarded, to carry out the research. Sometimes, this means doing the research themselves or subcontracting it out. If this profession interests you, familiarize yourself with the salaries, benefits, and working conditions at these organizations before mindlessly applying to these jobs. Some require you to work beyond normal business hours, often resulting in substantial unpaid overtime. And, unlike tenured academic jobs, employment in research consulting firms can be considerably more precarious.

Issues tied to subject matter specialization and one's alma mater are also important. Some research consulting organizations want highly specialized

DOI: 10.4324/9781003499145-28

subject matter experts. In contrast, others are fine with hiring people (with doctorates) who are generalists so that they can pivot from one research grant (or contract) to another, as the case may be. In terms of alma mater, many people think that just because you graduate from a particular university or department, like a highly ranked criminology/criminology one, you have great subject matter knowledge, exceptional training, and it imbues you with specific skills and proclivities. (This is also often the logic behind hiring people from Ivy League schools.)

Let's deconstruct this question further. Why would a government agency, research consulting firm, or even think tank want or need someone who has earned a PhD? In short, there is an assumption that individuals with this kind of qualification know about the latest scholarship, understand research design, can conduct research, and have both the skills and knowledge to judge the merits of different types of studies. This enables them to demonstrate to agencies why they should fund particular types of research.

It's also essential to consider the field in which you earned your PhD. If your doctorate is in history or the humanities, you might have a more challenging time securing a nonacademic job where criminology or criminal justice expertise is needed or wanted.

By all means, test the water, but be careful about giving up your tenured or tenure-track job for the allure of a government job with a criminal justice agency, a research consulting organization, or a think tank.

Also, remember that although crime isn't going away soon, and there may be less job security if you work for a research consulting company, rather than a government criminal justice agency, the latter are not immune from layoffs and downsizing. For example, during the initial months of the second Trump administration (2025), layoffs occurred at the federal level, including at the National Institute of Justice, the Department of Justice's principal research arm, and all grant-making activities were suspended.

Suggested reading

Ross, J. I. (2000). Grants-R-Us: Inside a federal grant making research agency. *American Behavioral Scientist*, *43*(10), 1704–1723.

Letter 25

IS BEING A CRIMINOLOGIST A GOOD WAY TO POSITIVELY IMPACT CRIMINAL JUSTICE POLICY AND PRACTICE?

Most criminologists want to do good. They want to ensure that neighborhoods, cities, states, and countries are safe, that police officers work within the bounds of the law, and that inmates coming out of prison are rehabilitated.

As Richard Sparks suggests,

> Criminology inherently deals with problems and actions that arouse powerful emotions: anger, indignation, fear, amongst others. It addresses the many complex ways in which we handle such problems and respond to such actions; it speaks to the appropriate use of power and the failures of those uses: punishment prevention, risk management, blame, accountability, forgiveness, restitution, and restoration. Inevitably underlying all those transactions are fundamental questions of politics: order, authority, legitimacy, justice. (2019, p. 165)

However, most criminologists also recognize that these noble goals are difficult to attain. They frequently ask about the impact that their teaching can have on their students (many of whom go on to be criminal justice practitioners) or their research on public policy and practice.

Some criminologists argue that the field's research "isn't causally certain." Others believe that criminologists are not in a good position to inform criminal justice policy and practice. Then again, others believe that our research is better than nothing.

The reason why this situation occurs is complicated. To begin with, despite the abundance of necessary and impactful (in terms of scholarly

DOI: 10.4324/9781003499145-29

citations it generates) research findings that scholars manage to publish, although some policymakers and practitioners read academic journals, a considerable number don't. Then again, even if a few influential people read and properly understand this material, it does not mean that they act upon this information. Why? They operate in a political context where the reward system does not favor developing and implementing new ideas into the criminal justice system but achieving power (i.e., political office), remaining in control, or other types of political influence. More specifically, there are many steps between being informed and doing something appropriate about an issue. One should never forget that policymakers typically make decisions based on their chances of maintaining their employment, being promoted, or in the case of politicians being elected or reelected (i.e., staying in power).

Criminologists should periodically reflect on which form of communication has the most significant impact on which audience: Rigorous scholarly research, opinion pieces that reach policymakers, or televised interviews addressing urgent criminology issues. Each serves a different function; scholarly research provides depth and empirical rigor, while media engagement offers immediacy and broader reach. To maximize their influence, criminologists might consider diversifying their communication strategies, writing for both academic and public audiences, and responding to media inquiries. This includes periodically writing articles or opinion pieces for newspapers and magazines, or answering requests from local, regional, and national news media when they want to interview an expert source.

Many academics, however, are reluctant to engage with general audiences, often prioritizing the researching and writing of publications aimed at their peers. Institutional incentives also discourage such engagement, as tenure and promotion committees typically value scholarly output over public outreach. Yet, mass media, particularly news outlets and social media platforms (e.g., Twitter/X, Facebook, Instagram), frequently shape public opinion more than academic research. Voters, policymakers, and practitioners rarely engage directly with scientific studies, relying instead on media content that is often simplified and sensationalized.

Given these realities, criminologists must weigh the trade-offs. While media appearances and opinion pieces can enhance visibility and influence, they also risk oversimplification or misrepresentation of complex findings. Scholarly research remains the bedrock of knowledge production, but its impact is limited if it does not reach those who can act on it. The challenge is not whether to engage with nonacademic audiences, but how to do so effectively, ensuring accuracy while maximizing influence.

More specifically, criminal justice policies, practices, and laws exist in a political context. Although rigorous peer-reviewed research may be conducted on criminological processes, criminal justice practices, and policies, they may be ignored. Why? Because the results are often not politically expedient, they will not help get a politician elected or reelected. For example, most scholarship on the death penalty indicates that this practice does not serve as a deterrent for people who are going to engage in murder. However, we still have the death penalty as an option in many states in the United States. Few politicians in those states will vote for the repeal of the death penalty in such jurisdictions because they fear they will not be elected or reelected.

Also, a politician may be beholden to a political party that supports or opposes a particular policy, practice, or law. Additionally, unions and special interest groups lobby and donate money to politicians to fund their campaigns. They do this because they want the politicians to support (i.e., pass) legislation supporting their policy preferences. Candidates running for office are almost always loath to vote against the wants and desires of these powerful influences. It would be political suicide if they did.

Alternatively, criminal justice agencies may not have sufficient resources to implement a new policy, practice, or law. These resources include money, skills, or a sufficient workforce. Finally, some new policies, practices, and laws may be poorly implemented. They may exist in our criminal codes, agency directives, policy and practice manuals, but the people responsible for implementing them do a bad job for various reasons.

In short, some criminologists are frustrated that the findings from their published research don't positively impact current criminal justice policy and practice. That being said, there are ways to tip the balance, but they are typically frustrating and resource-intensive. This involves drawing positive attention to one's work, including writing op-eds and blog posts, offering to serve as a subject matter expert to the news media (more about that later), and contacting the offices of policymakers and politicians (and actually speaking with them). Regardless of the subject specialization, many academics, regardless of the discipline, dislike engaging in these types of activities.

Nevertheless, criminologists may have a more significant impact not with policy, practice, and laws but on their students' understanding of crime, criminality, criminal justice, and most especially their current and future careers (and ultimately lives). Many students who enroll in criminology/criminal justice classes have limited views about this subject matter. This is predictable because they get the bulk of their information from the news, social media, and television shows which are predictably biased. Moreover, their family and neighborhood situations and socioeconomic status may narrowly circumscribe their lives and life experiences. By the time they graduate with a degree in criminology/criminal justice, hopefully, they have been exposed to the most important scholarly research on the challenges in the criminal justice system, the history of these issues, and this helps them to develop a critical understanding of criminal justice policies, practices, and laws and how they might be able to enable positive outcomes.

Suggested reading

Ashby, M. P. (2020). The open access availability of criminological research to practitioners and policymakers. *Journal of Criminal Justice Education*, *32*(1), 1–21.

Austin, J. (2003). Why criminology is irrelevant. *Criminology & Public Policy*, 2(3), 557–564.

Blomberg, T. G. (2019). Making a difference in criminology: Past, present, and future. *American Journal of Criminal Justice*, *44*(4), 670–688.

Boehme, H. M., Adams, I. T., Metcalfe, C., Leasure, P., & Nolan, M. S. (2024). Does scientific research change minds? Lining criminology and public perceptions of policy. *Criminology & Public Policy*, *23*(1), 201–224.

Petersilia, J. (1993). Policy relevance and the future of criminology. Presidential address. *Criminology*, *29*(1), 1–15.

Sherman, L. W. (2005). The use and usefulness of criminology, 1751–2005. Enlightened Justice and its failures. *ANNALS of the American Academy of Political and Social Science*, *600*(1), 115–135.

Sparks, R. (2019). Letter to a young criminologist (not unlike myself). In S. Pleysier & S. Vivijs (Eds.), *Brieven aan Jonge Criminologen* (pp. 161–165). Die Keure.

Wellford, C. F. (2009). Criminologists should stop whining about their impact on policy and practice. In N. A. Frost, J. D. Friedlich, & T. R. Clear (Eds.), *Contemporary issues in criminal justice policy: Policy proposals from the american society of criminology conference* (pp. 17–24). Wadsworth.

Worrall, J. L., & Gordon, Q. (2022). Is criminology & public policy "influential"? Answers from altmetrics. *Criminology & Public Policy*, *21*(4), 839–864.

Letter 26

I'M THINKING ABOUT WORKING ABROAD AS A CRIMINOLOGIST. IS THAT A GOOD IDEA?[1]

Picture yourself working as a criminologist in sunny Italy, Spain, or Portugal. You could regularly take long lunch breaks, eat delicious food, and drink great wine. Your weekends might include hanging out at the beach or hiking the mountains with your colleagues, friends, and loved ones. Besides the comparatively low cost of living, expenses like health care would be cheaper than in the United States.

Geiss (2014) writes about how many well-respected criminologists

> support cross-cultural endeavors. They point out that many generalizations in criminology and criminal justice are too parochial, stressing the pleasure of learning about foreign cultures. Indeed, the opportunity to travel and conduct research abroad is often mentioned as one of the fundamental delights of a criminological career. Several writers refreshingly cannot resist telling you where they have been, and some adventures associated with these excursions. Not least, they testify to the stimulation of colleagues around the globe who share their interest and enthusiasm for a common field of intellectual endeavor (p. xii).

Keep in mind that in some countries (especially European ones), there are no standalone departments of criminology/criminal justice. This means that, if hired by a university, you will typically be working in a department of sociology or a faculty of law. And some criminologists like this kind of arrangement, while others don't.

But will a foreign university (or even a criminal justice agency) hire you? And the short answer is that it depends on the situation. Can you speak

DOI: 10.4324/9781003499145-30

the language? Do you have citizenship, permanent residency, or another legal status that enables you to work? If it's a government agency that you want to work for, then citizenship or permanent residency may be necessary for security reasons. Some institutions will sponsor your visa (i.e., they will complete the paperwork, pay the filing charges, or hire a qualified legal professional to do this for you). These legal categories also affect access to public healthcare and tax obligations, so it's essential to understand your eligibility before applying for a job overseas.

Nevertheless, there are ways to increase the likelihood that your dream of working as a criminologist in a foreign country will come true. This includes, but isn't limited to, living in the country for a considerable period and, more significantly, earning your master's and/or your PhD in that country.

If you could earn one or both of these degrees overseas (outside of North America) at a respected university, this may be a great experience for several reasons. There are many well-respected master's and PhD programs in criminology/criminal justice in Canada, the United Kingdom, Australia, Belgium, Finland, Germany, Italy, the Netherlands, Norway, South Africa, and Sweden (and there are PhD programs in sociology and law, where one or more faculty members have specializations in criminology and criminal justice). The tuition costs are reasonable and, in some countries, free or almost free.

If you're a citizen or permanent resident of a low and middle-income (former British) Commonwealth country, you may be able to enroll in graduate degrees from universities in the United Kingdom and earn a dedicated scholarship. Suppose you're a citizen of a European Union country. In that case, you can take part in the Erasmus program, which enables you to earn your bachelor's, master's, or doctorate at any European Union university for practically free. Tuition for non-European Union citizens for master's and doctoral programs in countries such as Austria, the Czech Republic, Denmark, France, Germany, Norway, and Sweden is either low cost, mostly free, or completely free. All you need to do is pay for your living expenses.

But all things being equal, if you intend to return to Australia, Canada, New Zealand or the United States, it might be challenging to secure a job as an academic criminologist in these locations if your experience has only been in a non-Anglo-American country.

You may also be more marketable if you have produced a handful of impactful publications in your area of expertise and established and maintained a professional network in the country where you want to work. The question is, will there be much interest in what you specialize in? Again, these are things to figure out before subletting your apartment, selling your car and/or home (if needed), and buying your airplane ticket to your new country of residence

As you start addressing the real and imagined drawbacks, consider the following. While moving across the country is one thing, moving to a foreign country that requires at least a day of travel to get there is another. If you're single, you may have considerably more flexibility than someone with a partner and kids. However, if you have a family, you may need to uproot them. You may need to sell your residence and your possessions. Will you sell your most valuable assets at a loss? If you have a dog or a cat, they may be quarantined for an extended period before they are let into your new country.

In any case, be prepared for potentially lower salaries and different norms about productivity, collegiality, and the kinds of students, including their interests, commitment level, etc. Also, if you thought professor salaries in the United States, Canada, and Australia were low, wait until you find out how little they are paid in the United Kingdom, countries in Eastern Europe, and South America (where many professors need to supplement their income with part-time or full-time jobs). There is a reason why the cost of living is lower in many other countries. According to my colleague Kyle Mulroney, "Having worked across Europe, the UK, and now Australia, each system was so different. While there are no doubt similarities, working in these contexts may be difficult due to the institutional and cultural nuances."

Dmello (2024) outlines his story of taking a position at the University of Adelaide, covering "logistics, networks, career progression, and opportunity." He noted the increased use of Zoom meetings at after-hours times. Your Australian time is significantly ahead of the United States. Just as I'm settling into my evening routine, many of my Australian colleagues are just waking up. And if you're thinking of Australia or vice versa, the flights can be relatively expensive and brutal in terms of time in the air.

That's why my hat goes off to all my Australian and New Zealand colleagues who frequently travel to the United States to attend professional meetings here.

In the end, it might be wise to try to form relationships with criminologists in the country that interests you and to travel there as a visitor. Reach out to people at those universities, and, resources permitting, even do a sabbatical at a university in that country. Once at the new institution of higher education, do your due diligence, ask appropriate questions, and see if this place is really for you.

Note

1 Special thanks to Kyle Mulroney for sharing his insights on this letter/question.

Suggested reading

Dmello, J. (2024). Academia beyond borders: Experiences from moving across the world. *The Criminologist*, 50(5), 27–28.

Geis, G. (2014). Introduction. In G. Geis & M. Dodge (Eds.), *Lessons of criminology* (pp. ix–xiv). Routledge.

Letter 27

SHOULD ASPIRING CRIMINOLOGISTS GAIN CRIMINAL JUSTICE PRACTITIONER EXPERIENCE BEFORE, DURING, OR AFTER EARNING A DOCTORATE IN CRIMINOLOGY/CRIMINAL JUSTICE?

Practical experience in criminology or criminal justice has potential benefits, but it's value depends on what you did in the field to gain this understanding and how long you were there.

For instance, if your role was primarily administrative, such as making coffee for homicide detectives, the practical knowledge you gained might be minimal. Likewise, coding data for a criminology/criminal justice professor might be helpful. However, your time may be pointless if you do not understand how this activity fits into the larger study. Working in the field is valuable not only in terms of the knowledge and skills you might pick up, but also in the contacts you might make. On a related note, not everyone can translate what they learn in a professional setting to an academic setting or a specific subject field.

If you're already a criminologist, it's important to periodically get out of the ivory tower (i.e., the comfort of your office and lecture hall) and interact with criminal justice practitioners, victims of crime, policymakers, and politicians who are responding to crime, and if possible, current and former criminals. This provides an imperfect reality test for many of the ideas you have held for a respectable period.

Suppose you have gone straight through, from bachelor's through master's to doctorate, without summer jobs or internships in the criminology and criminal justice field. In that case, it's probably time to get some real-world experience, and doing this in a criminal justice agency may be a good option. This experience can be in the form of volunteering or a paid position in terms of summer or part-time jobs when you're in graduate school.

DOI: 10.4324/9781003499145-31

It's also necessary to explore things of interest or that give you pleasure other than what exists in the field of criminology/criminal justice. Whether that is a change in profession, a part-time job, a different location, travel, or a hobby, this can be done during intersession times (Christmas vacation, Spring break, or even a sabbatical). The change should help you put your current job, including your scholarship, into perspective. Unfortunately, this type of experimentation often happens when you have increased or competing obligations like a family, supporting aging parents, or managing mounting debts. In other words, there is rarely a convenient time to do all this.

Letter 28

IS IT BETTER FOR CRIMINOLOGISTS TO BE GENERALISTS OR SPECIALISTS?

One of the perennial questions in almost any field is, should you be a specialist or a generalist? And if you're a specialist, which subject should you focus on? This situation is no different in the field of criminology/criminal justice.

To begin with, there are no easy answers to this question.

Choosing to be a criminologist is, in fact, a step along the path of specialization. Initially and by necessity, your dissertation forces you to focus on a narrow topic or question. Not only do many academics (including criminologists) continue to research that subject for the balance of their careers, but they are generally happy with that specific focus focus and see no need to change topics. Although there are benefits to choosing this approach, including familiarity, convenience, and an absence of startup costs, there are also downsides. To begin with, there is no guarantee of a steady demand for this kind of research. More importantly, you risk becoming what some might call a "one-trick pony." This does not simply refer to your topic or question, but can also apply to your favored research methods. Before long, you may find yourself the person everyone tactfully avoids at conferences and social gatherings. At that point, you might start wondering how your deep expertise in "Crime prevention through environmental design" or "Reanalyzing Foucault's theory of the carceral system" plays out as dinner table conversation.

Let me explain further. Part of the answer to this question isn't so much about what criminological or criminal justice subject you might specialize in, but when in your career should you narrowly focus on one particular topic?

In order to secure an academic position, the ability to teach a variety of courses is essential. Over time, however, depending on the natural supply

DOI: 10.4324/9781003499145-32

and demand dynamics of the department you work in, it may be easier to teach the classes you want. If it's next to impossible to teach courses in the area you specialize in during the regular spring and fall semesters, you might be able to do this during the summer months or an interim session. Additionally, there may be retirements or loss of personnel in your department, opening the possibility for you to teach particular topics that interest you.

But, in the early part of your career, especially when you're on the job market, it might also be helpful to demonstrate to hiring committees that, in addition to the topic of your dissertation, you can teach in a variety of areas in criminology and criminal justice. And unless you know rather quickly that a specific position isn't for you, you don't want to talk the search committee out of offering you a job. This is why you might suggest that you're happy to teach large-enrollment classes that many professors dislike teaching, such as "Introduction to Criminology" or "Introduction to Criminal Justice," or smaller classes like "Research Methods" or "Statistics." In this manner, you make yourself look more appealing and willing to be a team player.

If you choose to specialize, it would be helpful to focus on a topic that is both interesting (that sustains your attention for a considerable period) and something that a significant number of people in the field of criminology/criminal justice care about. In other words, there is no sense in working hard on a topic that few specialists in the field are interested in. Certainly, timely topics have cachet, but it's essential to realize that there are startup costs, usually in terms of time. And by the time you have published half a dozen papers, wider interest in the subject may have waned.

That being said, sometimes the topics that criminologists focus on are chosen strategically, while others are done haphazardly. I've met several criminologists who like traveling to Europe or the Caribbean. At some point in their careers, they decided it would be worthwhile to do some scholarship in those locations to facilitate a frequent return to where they could combine work and pleasure. Others had partners who came from foreign countries, and they decided that conducting research in that location (and possibly contacts) might be helpful to facilitate a continuous return there.

Undoubtedly, there are so-called "hot topics," but this will be explored in the next letter.

Letter 29

WHAT ARE THE "HOT" RESEARCH TOPICS AND QUESTIONS IN CRIMINOLOGY/CRIMINAL JUSTICE?[1]

Periodically, students ask me what I consider to be the "hot topics" in criminology/criminal justice. Although I understand their curiosity and attempts to seek strategic advice, I always ask them what they mean by "hot topics" and why they believe focusing on these will benefit them.

Most students are looking for research ideas for their master's theses or doctoral dissertations, hoping that focusing on the "hot" subjects will open more doors for them. For master's students, a good topic might help them get accepted to a top PhD program. For doctoral students, it could mean securing an academic job in a "great" university or a position in a respectable criminal justice agency or research consulting firm.

However, there are several reasons why chasing hot topics might be ill-advised:

Relevance over time: By the time you complete your research, the topic might no longer be "hot."

Research quality: Focusing on a popular subject doesn't guarantee quality research or scholarship.

Supervisor expertise: Your supervisors might not have the expertise to guide you effectively.

Sustained interest: It's helpful to remain interested in the topic throughout your research; otherwise, the entire experience may feel like a long haul.

Instead of solely focusing on current trends, consider the following strategies:

Choose enduring, relevant, and impactful questions and problems within the discipline, such as gun control, youth violence, and prison overcrowding.

DOI: 10.4324/9781003499145-33

Understand the difference between broad topics (e.g., police use of force) and specific research questions (e.g., What factors lead to correctional officer deviance?).
Consider innovative solutions to long-standing problems (e.g., new protocols, technology, etc.). This approach makes your research relevant and increases your marketability to potential employers.

For example, during the COVID-19 pandemic (2020–2021), research on the virus's impact on the criminal justice system was heavily funded. Now that the pandemic has subsided, interest in this topic has waned. In contrast, enduring questions like the causes of youth violence remain relevant regardless of trends. Ultimately, while being aware of popular topics is functional, focusing on innovative solutions to long-standing issues has a greater chance of sustaining interest and making your research impactful and relevant in the long run, and making you attractive to potential employers.

In sum, remember that what is hot today may be lukewarm or even ice-cold tomorrow.

Note

1 An earlier version of this letter appeared as "What are the 'Hot' Research Topics and Questions in Criminology/Criminal Justice? July 20, 2024. https://jeffreyianross.com/what-are-the-hot-research-topics-and-questions-in-criminology-criminal-justice/

Letter 30

IS IT DIFFICULT FOR SOMEONE WHO HAS EARNED A DOCTORATE IN CRIMINOLOGY OR CRIMINAL JUSTICE TO LEAVE ACADEMIA, WORK FOR A CRIMINAL JUSTICE AGENCY, AND THEN RETURN TO ACADEMIA?

Unlike many professions (e.g., architecture, dentistry, medicine, etc.) or skilled trades (e.g., electricians, plumbers, HVAC technicians, etc.), which require regular license renewals, academia does not have such requirements. However, returning to academia after a break can still be challenging.

Before continuing, when I transitioned from academia to the National Institute of Justice, a handful of my colleagues, borrowing a well-known line from the movie *Star Wars*, suggested that I was "going over to the dark side." In other words, they believed that my research and approach to criminal justice policies and practice would be permanently and negatively tainted by this experience.

This kind of messaging gave me pause for concern, and I took it as a warning to remain mindful of potential biases not only that I might encounter but those I might unconsciously adopt. Despite my challenges with the organization (Ross, 2000), I ultimately found value in the experience. On the contrary, rather than corrupting my perspective, it allowed me to see how the sausage was made and provided me with lots of valuable contacts. I suspect that most productive researchers who temporarily work for criminal justice agencies such as the National Institute of Justice (USA), the Home Office (UK), the Solicitor General of Canada, or the Australian Institute of Criminology, before returning to academia or moving into private research consulting, benefit significantly from the insights they gain. But I digress.

Almost anything is possible within reason regarding employment in university settings. However, after leaving academia and working in the private or public sector, returning to a traditional position as a professor can be challenging. Remember that this situation isn't specific to criminology or criminal justice; the same fundamental dynamics occur regardless of the discipline.

DOI: 10.4324/9781003499145-34

Academic departments can be cautious about hiring individuals for full-time positions who have spent extended time outside academia. This reluctance often stems from concerns that applicants are simply looking to escape the demands of full-time nonacademic roles rather than pursuing an academic career out of genuine interest.

To overcome this skepticism, it's important to demonstrate a sustained commitment to teaching, research, and professional engagement. Academic units, whether programs, departments, colleges, or universities, generally want evidence that applicants are not only serious about returning to academia but also understand and are prepared for its core responsibilities: Teaching, research, and service.

Moreover, you must show that you bring something distinctive to the table. This could involve addressing a curricular gap, offering specialized knowledge, having experience with securing grants and contracts, or contributing useful professional networks and contacts.

In short, as with any job, you need to make a compelling case to prospective academic employers that you're not just qualified but are a strong match for the specific position, and that your transition is motivated by more than just a desire to leave your current role.

To strengthen your candidacy:

Maintain teaching experience: If possible, work as an adjunct while working in the public or private sector to demonstrate continued engagement with academia. I'm not suggesting teaching three classes between two different universities each semester. But teaching at least one class per year can be helpful.

Continue publishing in academic venues: Regular contributions to respected journals will keep your research profile active.

Join or stay involved in professional associations: Maintain membership (and perhaps leadership positions) in criminology or criminal justice learned societies and actively participate in conferences and events.

Network with other criminologists and criminal justice practitioners: Connections with faculty, researchers, and criminal justice professionals can provide valuable leads and recommendations.

Additionally, consider that available positions may not align with your preferred location. Be prepared to weigh the costs and benefits of relocating or commuting. The academic job market is increasingly competitive, but a strong, well-documented commitment to teaching, scholarship, and service can help tip the balance in your favor.

Suggested reading

Ross, J.I. (2000). Grants-R-Us: Inside a federal grant making research agency. *American Behavioral Scientist*, *43*(10), 1704-1723.

Letter 31

WHAT ARE THE JOB/CAREER PROSPECTS FOR INDIVIDUALS WITH DOCTORATES IN CRIMINOLOGY/CRIMINAL JUSTICE?

The job market, whether in academia, criminology, or the broader workforce, follows a cyclical pattern. Supply and demand fluctuate, meaning that while you may not secure a tenure-track job this year, next year's opportunities could be different. Understanding where to look for jobs, setting realistic expectations of academia and your role in it, and being adaptable are essential if you're on the job market.

Where to find job openings

Where do you find job openings in criminology/criminal justice? In the United States, there are three primary sources to consult. This includes the job postings on the American Society of Criminology and the Academy of Criminal Justice Sciences websites. Another is the job listings on www.highereducation.com, and the final is the *Chronicle of Higher Education*. Things become a little complicated if you want to look for a job in Europe. The Times Higher Education website is one of the first places to start if you are looking for an academic job overseas. For jobs in Canada, the website Academic Affairs is a must. If you're interested in a position with a department of sociology that might hire criminologists, look at the American Sociological Association website. Many of these websites will enable you to set up a job alert so you don't have to check them regularly, but keep in mind that many good jobs slip through the cracks when relying solely on these automated systems.

Although word of mouth might alert you to available jobs, unlike the situation in the private sector, all tenure-track jobs have official job postings. That does not mean that everyone has a fair shot at getting the job. There

DOI: 10.4324/9781003499145-35

are normative aspects in any field that shape the decision-making of selecting candidates to be interviewed, who gets a campus visit, and who gets a job offer.

For example, being in a department as a grad student may provide you with adjunct or part-time teaching or research positions. However, don't be lulled into thinking that serving as an adjunct, part-timer, or had a one or two-year contract in a department gives you an inside track when a full-time position becomes available. Hiring committees are fickle beasts, and although you might apply and may even be granted a formal interview, when push comes to shove, the hiring committee is just as likely to choose someone other than you and to make a recommendation to the dean to extend a contract to them.

Unrealistic expectations

Many senior academics are insulated from the broader realities of higher education and the job market. And criminologists are no different. This becomes especially apparent at conferences, where the same recycled ideas, rooted in outdated frameworks, circulate with little innovation or engagement with current challenges and the scholarship to support this.

Some faculty settle into a routine: They teach their courses, meet only the basic requirements, and complain about the university system without actively seeking change. This may stem from learned helplessness, shaped by years of bureaucratic roadblocks. At one point, these same faculty may have proposed new initiatives to benefit their students, department, college, or the university, but then they found their ideas buried in bureaucratic red tape, co-opted by others, or dismissed outright. Over time, the frustration of navigating institutional inertia can lead even the most ambitious instructors and professors to disengage.

At the same time, many graduate students and faculty overestimate their value to their institutions. They assume their research, teaching, or service makes them indispensable, failing to recognize how easily universities adapt, replace, or restructure when budgets shrink and priorities shift.

Of course, academia isn't unique in fostering complacency or workplace toxicity; these issues exist in any profession. But in an era of financial uncertainty and shifting institutional priorities, failing to recognize one's replaceability can be costly.

Adaptability

Rather than assume job security or institutional loyalty, academics, especially those seeking tenure-track positions, should remain adaptable. The market changes, and so should they. If the only jobs available for the last two years are teaching policing, and all you've trained for is corrections, then you should consider how you can bridge into this subject.

Suggested reading

Applegate, B. K., Cable, C. R., & Sitren, A. H. (2009). Academia's most wanted: The characteristics of desirable academic job candidates in criminology and criminal justice. *Journal of Criminal Justice Education, 20*(1), 20–39.

Burns, R. G., & Kinkade, P. (2008). Finding fit: The nature of a successful faculty employment search in criminal justice, *Journal of Criminal Justice*, *36*(4), 372–378.

Sitren, A. H., & Applegate, B. K. (2012). Hiring criminology and criminal justice academics: The perceived importance of job candidates' attributes. *Journal of Criminal Justice Education*, *23*(1), 23–40.

Letter 32

IS IT EASIER TO BE HIRED AS A PROFESSOR OF CRIMINOLOGY/ CRIMINAL JUSTICE THAN IN OTHER ALLIED FIELDS?

To begin with, at least in criminology/criminal justice, there are more jobs available for adjuncts and one-year contract positions than for tenure-line, assistant, associate, and full professors. And at the higher academic ranks, there is an expectation that not only will you have a stellar academic reputation but that you have a track record of securing external grants (or contracts), program management and building, and supervising graduate students.

In some respects, due to supply and demand dynamics, securing a tenured or tenure-track job in criminology/criminal justice may be easier than in several related disciplines. In some years, job openings in criminology/criminal justice outnumber those in anthropology, political science, or sociology. However, protectionism within criminology/criminal justice has increased, leading to hiring preferences for candidates with doctorates specifically in the field rather than those from allied disciplines.

If your PhD is in another specialization, consider whether you would feel more comfortable in a criminology/criminal justice department or one aligned with your original discipline. For example, sociology has a complex relationship with criminology. As Geis (2015) observes,

> Criminology and criminal justice split off from sociology where they are regarded… as waifs, tolerated because they kept enrollments high. Their later structural independence demonstrated enough that the problems they addressed often were considerably more significant than the more esoteric menus offered by their parent discipline. Indeed, as sociology has tended to wane, criminology and criminal justice studies have flourished (p. xiii).

DOI: 10.4324/9781003499145-36

While sociology departments often seek faculty with expertise in criminology and/or criminal justice, they typically require candidates to hold a doctorate in sociology for tenure-track/tenured positions. This limitation means candidates from disciplines other than sociology may have fewer chances to be hired in these settings. On the other hand, some departments (e.g., cultural studies), regardless of the social science discipline, may employ interdisciplinary faculty and be more amenable to considering individuals with a criminology/criminal justice background because they believe it adds academic diversity to the kind of program they want to build and maintain.

Given academia's hiring dynamics, job seekers should cast a wide net in their applications while making a compelling case for how their expertise aligns with a department's needs. This requires thorough research into each department's faculty composition, teaching priorities, and research focus. Understanding the institution's key figures, student demographics, and academic culture is crucial. Many applicants fail to do this, resulting in generic applications that are quickly dismissed by hiring committees.

Ultimately, strategic career planning and a well-researched approach to job applications will improve the likelihood of securing a desirable academic position in criminology/criminal justice or a related field.

Suggested reading

Geis, G. (2015). Introduction, In Geis, G & Dodge, M. (Eds.) *Lessons of Criminology*, (pp. ix-xiv), Routledge.

Letter 33

HOW MUCH MONEY COULD I EXPECT TO MAKE IF I BECOME A CRIMINOLOGIST?

Answering this question is complex. Why? Salary figures fluctuate over time and can quickly become outdated. In fact, most scholarship on criminologist employment trends is obsolete (e.g., Gould & del Carmen, 2011). Instead of relying on fixed numbers, explore sources like state salary databases (for public institutions), job platforms like Indeed or Glassdoor, and academic salary surveys published by professional organizations. If you work at a state university, yours and your colleagues' salaries may be publicly available. That said, working as an academic criminologist is generally not a high-paying career, so it's essential to consider other factors when evaluating job opportunities, such as job security, benefits, work-life balance, colleagues, cost of living, and the intrinsic rewards of the profession.

Suggested reading

Gould, L. A., Fowler, S. K., & del Carmen, A. (2011). Faculty employment trends in criminology and criminal justice. *Journal of Criminal Justice Education*, 22(2), 247–266.

DOI: 10.4324/9781003499145-37

Letter 34

IS EARNING A BACHELOR'S, MASTER'S, OR DOCTORATE IN CRIMINOLOGY/CRIMINAL JUSTICE A GOOD STEPPING STONE TO BECOMING A CRIMINAL LAWYER?

Becoming a lawyer, at least in the United States or Canada, requires admission to law school and passing the bar exam in the state or province where you intend to practice. Additional requirements, such as "character and fitness" assessments, may also apply.

In the United States and Canada, law school admission typically requires completing a bachelor's degree with a high grade point average, high scores on standardized tests like the Law School Admissions Test (LSAT), and producing a convincing personal statement. In countries like the United Kingdom, most European countries and Australia, and New Zealand on the other hand, high school graduates with sufficiently high grades can enter law school directly.

To begin with, no publicly available data or study suggests that law school applicants stand a better chance of admission if they have an undergraduate, master's, or doctoral degree in criminology/criminal justice. Nonetheless, I suspect that law school admissions departments might find candidates with graduate degrees (e.g., master's or doctorate) in criminology/criminal justice somewhat unusual. Then again, you would probably stand a better chance of gaining admittance to law school if some or more of your classes at the undergraduate level were in criminology than someone who completed their undergraduate degree in a vastly different subject (e.g. Fine Arts).

Keep in mind that other dynamics can occur. After a handful of years working as a criminologist, you may discover that this job isn't for you and decide to explore law school. Be careful what you ask for. You're probably older, wiser, and perhaps still in debt from your graduate school years.

DOI: 10.4324/9781003499145-38

Maybe you can go to law school for free because of an educational benefit provided by your university. Still, you would probably have to attend at least initially part-time during the fall and spring, and maybe full-time in the summer. The law school at your university or where you can take advantage of an educational benefit may run a night law school, which may be more conducive to your schedule. One of the advantages of this model is that you could go to law school part-time first and then decide later about switching careers.

Remember, however, that not all law schools are organized this way. In other words, many of them require full-time studies, which may mean either taking a leave of absence from your job as a professor or quitting your job and the implications that ensue from this decision.

Regardless of which path you take, the additional knowledge about the law you gain should lead you to become a more informed criminologist.

PART IV

In the trenches

Instruction/teaching, research, and service[1]

Note

1 Unlike the other sections in this book, this one is divided into three subsections.

DOI: 10.4324/9781003499145-39

Instruction/Teaching

Letter 35

HOW WOULD YOU DESCRIBE THE TYPICAL CRIMINOLOGY/ CRIMINAL JUSTICE STUDENT?

Although I've taught classes in political science and sociology, most of my teaching experience has been in criminology and criminal justice. I've also lectured at undergraduate and graduate levels in Canada, Chile, France, Germany, Italy, and the United Kingdom, though my primary teaching has been within U.S. institutions. This has also included instruction at private and public university settings. Despite varying student populations across these disciplines, countries, and academic levels, each with its cultural expectations and approaches to learning, I've observed several trends among criminology and criminal justice students that transcend national boundaries. So, who are your typical criminology/criminal justice students?

General student characteristics

Motivations

Criminology/criminal justice students have a variety of reasons why they want to earn a degree in this field. These motivations vary based on several factors. One of the most important is the type of degree (i.e., bachelor's, master's, or doctorate) they seek. Some students may have done poorly in the classes they took in other disciplines and believe they can succeed or pass the courses in the discipline of criminology/criminal justice. Even if criminology/ criminal justice students are not practitioners, many would like to be. Some applied to criminal justice agencies during or right after high school or community college but, for one reason or another, were not hired or decided to delay working for these organizations until they earned a bachelor's. A few of these same students believe that earning a bachelor's or a graduate degree

DOI: 10.4324/9781003499145-40

in criminology/criminal justice will enable them to secure a job with a criminal justice agency, a specific criminal justice organization, and perhaps at a higher rank or pay level than they would have with simply a high school or community college diploma. Meanwhile, others think that completing a BA in criminology/criminal justice will increase their odds of getting into law school. Finally, many students want to be victim advocates in or for a criminal justice or social work agency and believe that a bachelor's degree in criminology/criminal justice will assist them in this process.

Many students major in criminology/criminal justice because they believe the subject is relevant to the "real world" and want to be criminal justice practitioners. To them, being a practitioner enables them to work with, meet, and help people. They also anticipate that the work will be interesting and exciting and that positions in this field offer opportunities for advancement, promotion, job security, respect, and attractive retirement packages (Krimmel & Tartaro, 1999; Courtright & Mackey, 2004).

Demographics and family situation

A substantial number of the students who enroll in classes in this discipline come from working-class or lower middle-class backgrounds. They may even be the first in their family to attend a university. Why is this the case? Statistically, few middle-class students want to become criminal justice practitioners. And if their parents are paying the tuition, they generally don't want their children to work as police, correctional, or probation officers. On the other hand, some students believe earning a degree in criminology/criminal justice would be a good stepping stone to becoming a criminal lawyer (more is said about this in another letter).

Since most departments of criminology/criminal justice are located in state schools (i.e., publicly funded institutions), the racial, ethnic, and gender distribution of students typically mirrors the local demographics. If you teach in a big city in the United States, then many of your students will be African American or Hispanic, and a significant share from immigrant backgrounds too. If you teach in a rural area, lots of your students probably grew up in small towns, long-established local communities and on farms.

Some criminology/criminal justice students are also single parents, disproportionately single moms and occasionally single dads. Others share custody of their children with an ex-partner, complicating childcare arrangements. On more than one occasion, I've had students bring their young children to class. Additionally, some of your students' children may have special needs, which compete for their attention. Your students may also be primary caregivers to their aging, elderly, or disabled parents or siblings.

Work situation

Many of your students will have full-time jobs, while others will be employed part-time, and a handful will have both full-time and part-time positions. Some will be working on campus as security officers, in the library, or doing clerical work. Others will work typical 9–5 positions, whereas a number may be on night shifts or rotating schedules.

Over the years, my students have held a variety of jobs. Many are gig workers. Some are employed in the food service industry as hosts at restaurants, counter staff, bartenders, baristas, waitpersons, servers, prep cooks, etc. Other students have jobs in retail as salespersons, cashiers, stock clerks, and loss prevention officers. Several work in food delivery (e.g., DoorDash, etc.) or as rideshare drivers (e.g., Uber, Lyft, etc.). A few are employed in landscaping or groundskeeping, and others are employed in hospitals as porters, clerks, nurse aides, etc. Some work for the Transportation Security Administration at airports, screening and assisting passengers going through security.

You will also encounter many students who were or are in the military, the reserves, or the National Guard. To varying degrees, these entities often help cover tuition and book costs for service members. However, this benefit can be a hassle for them at the beginning of the semester as they wait for their paperwork to be processed.

Other students have had jobs in the criminal justice or legal system, ranging from dispatchers in criminal justice agencies, to law enforcement, corrections, probation, or parole officers, and even reentry advocates. In the legal system, they could have worked as paralegals, legal secretaries, or on behalf of a judge.

In addition, I've had a handful of "failed" criminal justice practitioners among my students. This includes those who washed out of the police or corrections academy or were terminated for cause after some time on the job. Likewise, many of your students may be justice-involved, and a few may have been formerly incarcerated or have loved ones or relatives who have been behind bars.

A handful of students have done internships with criminal justice agencies. And depending on what they did during this time, the internship may have given them a sense of what it's like to be a criminal justice practitioner.

Another issue to consider is how much your students know beyond the city, county or suburb in which they grew up. Short of a visit to Disneyland with their parents or a high school trip to the state capital or maybe even Washington, DC, many of them have not journeyed outside of their state. Some of your students may not have traveled outside of the country where they were born. This means that the content of your lectures and interactions should consider these contextual issues when trying to teach the subtleties of a topic.

In general, master's students in criminal justice programs are typically practitioners. Many are police, correctional, probation, or parole officers, and hold mid-level ranks in these organizations. Their primary motivation for pursuing a master's degree isn't because they have an innate curiosity about the causes of crime or criminal justice organizational efficiency, but rather they want career advancement (i.e., move up the chain of command). For them, gaining insight into these areas is a byproduct of their studies. Also, the degree to which they pursue such engagement often depends on both individual interests and program structure.

On the other hand, doctoral students are usually either considering an academic career or believe that a PhD will enhance their prospects in the research division of a criminal justice agency. Those on the enforcement side may view the degree as a bridge to assuming a leadership role, such as police chief, warden, or a high-level management position in headquarters or with a state or federal criminal justice agency.

Challenges faced by students and instructors

What does this mean? Your students may lead busy and complicated lives. They may show up to class late, stressed, exhausted, burned out, and distracted. Students who fit this description are not ideal to teach and have challenges learning. All this to say is that the class you're teaching may not be at the top of your students' priority list.

This situation has made it more difficult for instructors who teach in the context of Zoom classes or asynchronously. Concerning the first modality, some of your students may be multitasking while being in class, including working full or part-time, driving their vehicles, taking public transportation, preparing dinner, eating a meal, cleaning up, doing childcare, or snuggling with their partners while comfortably relaxing on their beds. You may find yourself staring at a zoom screen where half your students are logged in, but their cameras are off. While some instructors don't mind teaching in this situation, others will find this incredibly frustrating. However, criminology and criminal justice instructors are not alone in experiencing this kind of situation. I try to tell my students that if they feel uncomfortable or shy about sharing their screens in a classroom setting, then they should probably seriously reconsider becoming a criminal justice practitioner where they will be interacting with the public including people in crisis and criminals on a daily basis, where face-to-face communication is the basis of the job.

Many students enter criminology and criminal justice courses with limited knowledge of American history, geography, and law. They may also find these content areas irrelevant to criminology/criminal justice. This gap makes it challenging to teach key concepts effectively. In the past, I began my introduction to the contemporary criminal justice system class by having students take a scaled-down version of the American citizenship test. However, after a few years, I discontinued the exercise because students performed poorly, and the experience proved more discouraging than beneficial. Many of my students' limited understanding of the U.S. Constitution is particularly concerning, as criminal justice practitioners must protect the civil liberties of the individuals they encounter in daily in their work.

Sometimes, teaching my students also feels like I'm watching an episode of *Saturday Night Live Weekend Update* with a comedy bit by Secondhand News correspondent Anthony Crispino (played by actor Bobby Moynihan). Although I'm pleased that students are actively participating, some of them confidently present misinformation, and I must respond politely while suppressing disbelief.

Implications for teaching

Despite this picture, many undergraduate and graduate criminology/criminal justice students are exceptionally talented, often seeing things that many experts would overlook and generating ideas and solutions to crime and criminal justice challenges that exceed my expectations. Their insights push the boundaries of what I, as an instructor, thought possible in the classroom. However, you will also encounter students who seem underprepared for university-level work. This variation is often more noticeable in universities with open admissions policies, and practices where a diverse range of students, many of whom may not have had access to robust educational resources, are accepted without standardized test scores (e.g., SAT).

Although teaching this latter type of student can be challenging, one must remember that these individuals often bring unique perspectives and potential that may not be immediately apparent. The goal for educators lies not in questioning how these students were admitted or criticizing them but in finding ways to support their academic growth. By fostering an inclusive environment, directing them to campus resources that offer tutoring, mentoring, study, or writing services and skills, and implementing differentiated teaching strategies, we can assist all students, regardless of their starting point, in reaching their full potential.

Suggested reading

Courtright, K. E., & Mackey, D. A. (2004). Job desirability among criminal justice majors: Exploring relationships between personal characteristics and occupational attractiveness. *Journal of Criminal Justice Education*, *15*(2), 311–326.

Disha, I. Eren, C., & Leyro, S. (2021). People you care about in and out of the system: The impact of arrest on CJ's major choice and career motivations. *Journal of Criminal Justice Education*, *31*(1), 60–89.

Eren, C. P., Leyro, S., & Disha, I. (2019). It's personal: The impact of victimization on motivations and career interests among criminal justice majors at diverse urban colleges. *Journal of Criminal Justice Education*, *30*(4), 510–535.

Krimmel, J. T., & Tartaro, C. (1999). Career choices and characteristics of criminal justice undergraduates. *Journal of Criminal Justice Education*, *10*(2), 277–289.

Letter 36

WHAT IS THE BEST TYPE OF INSTRUCTION IN THE FIELD OF CRIMINOLOGY/CRIMINAL JUSTICE?

One perennial question is how best to teach undergraduate and graduate criminology/criminal justice students.

Undoubtedly, there is a time and place for almost all types of instruction. But criminology and criminal justice programs face unique constraints that shape their teaching approaches. Large undergraduate class sizes and limited availability of teaching assistants often lead instructors and professors to rely on lecture-based formats for content delivery. To assess student learning in these environments, many instructors use multiple-choice and short-answer examinations, sometimes supplemented by brief essays, assignments, and term papers.

Remember that many of your students are nontraditional adult learners. A good number will be concrete, nonabstract thinkers. Often, they don't want to, or have difficulty, "thinking outside the box" (i.e., finding creative solutions to relatively complex problems). Many believe that in the field of criminology/criminal justice, there is one correct answer for each question or challenge they face, and they may prefer to be told what to do because they do not want to make mistakes, fear being sanctioned, or lose their jobs. Since many decisions in the criminal justice field are life-and-death ones, engaging in creative problem-solving is often not part of their approach. Additionally, some instructors are lazy, burnt out, or overburdened by large class sizes and workloads, making it difficult to give each student the individualized attention they need.

This presents a dilemma for instructors and potential employers. Although criminal justice agencies want employees to follow orders, given the diversity of the situations they may find themselves in and the people they deal with,

DOI: 10.4324/9781003499145-41

they almost always want them to think and act rationally and creatively. (A great example of this trend is the problem-oriented policing movement, where patrol officers are expected to consult community members and leaders and devise plans together to minimize crime in these environments.)

Teaching materials

Numerous instructors and professors structure the subjects that they are going to cover around the content of textbooks that they assign to their classes. In this case, each unit or lecture closely follows the content and chronological order of the text. With others, the professor "drives the train," (i.e., the instructor selects the content for each unit or lecture) and the textbook "comes along for the ride" (i.e., the textbook assists students understand the instructor's unit of lecture). Regardless, as an instructor or professor, your inbox will typically contain a substantial number of notifications from publishers about new books they are selling. You may even have textbook sales representatives who make the rounds, going from office to office, trying to interest you in adopting old and new books their company publishes (less so since COVID-19 and the advent of online teaching). Short of these two communication channels, publishers will attend national and some regional criminology/criminal justice conferences, bringing their wares. Understanding the utility of this material and recognizing that some texts are better than others is important. Also, realize that many of your students don't like to read and especially dislike reading journal articles. Thus, a text is sometimes preferred in these situations.

Preparation

Another significant issue for instructors is staying informed about current events related to criminal justice, as this information can be valuable not only to them but to students. At a minimum, regularly read the local newspaper or follow local news, with particular attention to crime and justice issues, so you can speak knowledgeably about relevant developments.

Evaluation methods

Instructors must acknowledge that their job is to impart information to their students and then determine if they have adequately learned the material and can apply it meaningfully. Sometimes, however, there is a big disconnect between these two issues. In addition to traditional methods of evaluating students, another type of assignment requires students to interview a criminal justice professional (e.g., correctional officer, probation officer, courtroom clerk) or a formerly incarcerated person. This can force your students out of their comfort zones and make them confront some of the stereotypes they have developed and currently hold.

Over the years, presenting students with scenarios and having them role-play has been a good way to teach or sensitize them to particular issues in the field. This allows them to learn the material more deeply. This kind of pedagogy forces students to think through the implications of their choices. It also works well in group situations where other students diplomatically criticize their fellow class members' decisions.

Content

Part of what many criminologists do, particularly in the introductory classes, is spend a considerable amount of time debunking myths. Again, some textbooks are structured in this manner. And just like the previously mentioned student who expresses a desire to be a criminal profiler, you can see throughout the semester, students who initially indicated that they wanted to be police officers or criminal defense lawyers getting a little depressed. They are learning that the field of criminology/criminal justice is not as simple as they thought, or as depicted by popular media. They learn, for example, that sometimes, despite their good intentions, law enforcement officers are hampered by organizational realities, etc.

Another critical issue is your students' demeanor and how this affects their amenability to learn. The most notable issue here is the preponderance of authoritarian personality traits among male undergraduate criminal justice students, particularly at the lower level of education (Owen & Wagner, 2008; Hurley & Hurley, 2015). This kind of orientation can present palpable difficulties for instructors. But it also means that with more education, particularly at the upper levels, these individuals tend to dissipate these types of beliefs as they become more educated. It's unclear if the education is more criminology and criminal justice courses, but it seems to be a belief among academic criminologists.

Some students struggle with writing clearly and coherently. This issue is not confined to formal assignments like essays and research papers; it often extends to everyday communication, including emails. This presents another serious challenge, especially for those pursuing careers in criminal justice, where precise and professional report writing is essential.

Equally important is oral communication. Criminal justice practitioners frequently engage in interviews, briefings, and courtroom testimony. For this reason, I strongly encourage students to give oral presentations in class as part of their training. Understandably, some students push back, often citing shyness or discomfort with public speaking. When this happens, I ask them to seriously consider how they expect to succeed in a profession that demands clear, confident written and spoken communication.

Finally, American universities (and I suspect most others operating in advanced industrialized democracies) are increasingly moving toward online instruction, at least at the undergraduate level. This format has advantages and disadvantages, and students, instructors, and administrators may have wildly different opinions on whether they like it. This presents numerous challenges for criminology and criminal justice instructors and their students. Integrating many of the techniques mentioned above is difficult, but not impossible, in the online environment.

Suggested reading

Greek, C. E. (1995). Using active learning strategies in teaching criminology: A personal account. *Journal of Criminal Justice Education*, *6*(1), 153–164.

Hurley, D. C., & Henderson Hurley, M. (2015). Education alone isn't the answer: The specter of right-wing authoritarianism for criminal justice majors at three institutions. *Journal of Criminal Justice Education,* 26(4), 371–389.

Owen, S. S., & Wagner, K. (2008). The specter of authoritarianism among criminal justice majors. *Journal of Criminal Justice Education*, *19*(1), 30–53.

Ross, J. I. (2001, March 2). Why writing well is important for criminal justice practitioners. Retrieved March 7, 2025, from https://jeffreyianross.com/why-writing-well-is-important-for-criminal-justice-practitioners/

Letter 37

MY STUDENTS AND I FEEL UNEASY DISCUSSING CONTROVERSIAL, IDEOLOGICAL, AND POLITICAL TOPICS IN CLASS. WHAT CAN I DO?

Many of the most pressing issues in the American contemporary criminal justice system, such as the death penalty, sentencing disparities, and prison abolition, are inherently contentious. Criminology/criminal justice instructors and professors who avoid political discussions or shy away from controversial and complex topics do their students a disservice. Failing to address these topics in a classroom setting does not mean that this subject matter lacks importance; it only deprives students of the opportunity to critically engage with the real-world complexities they will encounter in the field. These discussions touch on personal morals, ethics, and philosophy, all great topics to touch on during classroom discussions.

Balancing perspectives in the classroom is one of the central challenges for instructors and professors, but it's essential for cultivating informed critical thinking. Discomfort is often a sign of that the topic/s need to be addressed in a thoughtful manner. If students and faculty find themselves unsettled by specific discussions, that isn't a failure of pedagogy; it's a sign that deep, meaningful engagement should be taking place.

In short, avoiding controversial topics in the field does not make the criminal justice classroom a neutral space; it simply leaves critical issues unexamined. Ultimately, criminal justice education isn't just about knowledge transmission but about preparing students to think critically, engage in informed debate, and navigate a complex, often contentious field with intellectual integrity.

DOI: 10.4324/9781003499145-42

Teaching with transparency

In my classes, I address these complex topics as objectively as possible while being as transparent as possible about my perspectives on their subjective elements. I typically do this by revealing a little about my experiences, including how my beliefs may have changed over time and why. I also give a short lecture on ideology and philosophy, usually early in the semester, including what these topics refer to, the different types, how it influences criminal justice policies, their relationship to traditional political parties, and why it matters in our discussions. Some students immediately grasp the role of ideology and philosophy in shaping criminal justice policies and practices, and the laws debated and sometimes passed in legislatures, while others struggle with it. But even when comprehension varies, introducing these concepts helps lay the foundation for critical engagement.

There is no such thing as a value-free criminology or criminal justice. This does not mean instructors should impose their views or demand ideological conformity. Instead, it means that all perspectives, including our own, should be examined critically. Topics like incarceration in general, and the death penalty, life without parole, and justice system reform, in particular, require nuanced analysis, not simplistic conclusions. Students should be encouraged to challenge their assumptions and diplomatically debate those of their peers, instructors, and the subject matter we expose them to. This extends to the assigned readings and audio-visual materials that instructors ask their students to consult.

Another important challenge is addressing the stereotypes and myths that students bring to the subject. As Calaguari and Muzzatti (2022) note,

> This common-sense view of crime is based on numerous problematic assumptions, stereotypes, and falsehoods. What at first seems an impediment to critical learning isn't an obstacle but presents an opportunity to engage in a transgressive pedagogy, in a critical rethinking that engages the students' passionate interest in all things criminal. (p. 266)

One prominent example is the street crime versus suite crime debate: Most undergraduate students assume that street criminals commit the majority of crimes. This misconception offers a valuable opening to explore broader issues, such as race, ethnicity, social class, and the privileges that shape who has access to certain benefits in society.

Connecting opinions to empirical

Regardless, opinions must be grounded in empirical evidence. Criminal justice educators must ensure that students understand the difference between personal beliefs, anecdotal observations, and conclusions drawn from empirical research. This is why students and instructors should know what peer review research is, how it is conducted, and what happens when policies and practices are implemented without the benefit of consulting this before hand. It is especially significant in an era of widespread misinformation, social media amplificaton of this material, and public debates often driven by ideology rather than data to understand these subtleties. Reinforcing the importance of peer-reviewed research and sound methodology helps students develop the analytical skills to navigate these issues thoughtfully.

Suggested reading

Colaguori, C., & Muzzatti, S. L. (2022). Teaching and doing anti-criminology: An autoethnography of transgressive pedagogies. *Contemporary Justice Review*, *25*(3–4), 256–270.

Williams, E. J., & Robinson, M. (2004). Ideology and criminal justice: Suggestions for a pedagogical model. *Journal of Criminal Justice Education*, *15*(1), 373–392.

Research

Letter 38

CAN A PERSON BE AN ACADEMIC CRIMINOLOGIST WITHOUT CONDUCTING OR PUBLISHING SCHOLARLY RESEARCH?

Sure, but this will limit your employment and promotion options. Criminologists who do not conduct scholarly research often find that the only viable academic jobs are at community colleges. Many criminologists are perfectly happy with this kind of work environment. Another possible outcome is securing a succession of one- to three-year contract positions with criminology/criminology departments. However, the likelihood of continued employment when a tenured position becomes available is slim if the candidate has not demonstrated sufficient scholarship.

What often happens, however, is that entry level professors conduct scholarly research for a while. Once they earn tenure (when promoted to associate professor status), then they either cut back on their research productivity or not do it at all. You may be asking why universities even require professors to do research. There are many reasons, but one primary justification is the belief that this work can help maintain or enhance a university's prestige (and attract more student enrollments, government funding, etc.). Additionally, there is an expectation that professors will secure one or more grants that will underwrite their salary and pay for one or more graduate assistants to assist with this research, thereby helping to train the next generation. There is an additional belief that, by doing research in your field, you will be able to learn things that you can pass on to your students.

DOI: 10.4324/9781003499145-43

Letter 39

IS ONE RESEARCH METHOD BETTER THAN ANOTHER FOR CRIMINOLOGY/ CRIMINAL JUSTICE RESEARCH?

Although criminologists might take comfort in the fact that this challenge isn't specific to criminology or criminal justice, another frequent question in the field is whether one research method is better than another.

While certain research methods, such as crime rate analysis and survey-based studies, and research designs, like quasi-experimental and longitudinal, are widely employed in criminological research, others remain underutilized within traditional criminology and criminal justice scholarship. These include legal analysis, historical inquiry, and experimental methodologies. The limited use of experimental methods, in particular, may be attributed to complex legal, moral, and ethical concerns surrounding the manipulation of variables in real-world justice settings.

Choosing a research method is like selecting the right tool for a specific job: Effectiveness depends on fit. Just as you wouldn't use a power saw to drive in a nail, or a sledgehammer when a standard hammer would suffice, methodological mismatch or overreach can lead to confusing results. For example, attempting to survey active bank robbers may not only be logistically difficult and potentially dangerous, but it also raises serious concerns about data reliability, as participants may be unwilling or unable to provide truthful responses.

That being said, there is a constant low-intensity battle between quantitative and qualitative researchers. Each side often accuses the other of lacking rigor: Quantitative scholars may dismiss qualitative work as anecdotal, while qualitative researchers frequently argue that quantitative studies focus too narrowly on easily measurable topics (where data is easily accessible) often at the expense of more meaningful or complex questions. These

DOI: 10.4324/9781003499145-44

criticisms aren't confined to criminologists; even casual observers sometimes echo them.

For example, in qualitative research, autoethnography is often disparaged by quantitative researchers as biased. This reflects a lack of understanding of how to properly conduct it. Likewise, many criminologists who claim their work is autoethnographic are simply engaging in story-telling, some of which are akin to war stories, rather than rigorous autoethnography. In short, the finished product does not conform to the basic definition (i.e., systematic observations over a specified period of time). That being said, mixed methods are underappreciated. Properly conducting this kind of research requires a great deal of skill .

Ultimately, the question that an investigator wants to answer usually determines the research method to be utilized. In principle, you should be well-versed in numerous research methods. This way, you can take advantage of a lot more opportunities. How do you do this? Hopefully, your undergraduate and graduate student classes have exposed you to and adequately prepared you to tackle a variety of research methods. Maybe you gained some valuable experience during your master's degree if you wrote a thesis, or your doctorate if you wrote a dissertation. Alternatively, you might be able to team up with someone with the skills you need.

Nonetheless, if your ultimate goal is to be published in *Criminology*, the flagship journal of the American Society of Criminology, it would be wise to see what kind of methodologies the research published in this journal utilizes and then try to emulate it. In other words, a highly qualitative paper will not stand much chance of being reviewed or accepted by a journal that disproportionately publishes quantitative research, and vice versa.

Another issue criminologists often face involves navigating institutional review boards (IRBs). Because criminological research frequently involves observing or asking populations such as incarcerated individuals, perpetrators of crime, or others involved in the criminal justice system, IRBs may impose strict oversight to ensure ethical standards are maintained. Universities, in turn, may be concerned about potential legal or reputational risks associated with research involving these groups (Ross et al., 2000). As a result, obtaining approval for fieldwork or ethnographic research can be especially difficult, potentially limiting the scope and depth of criminological inquiry.

In the end, the issue for researchers is not what the best methodology is to answer the question they want to answer, but what the best fit is.

Suggested reading

Buckler, K. (2008). The quantitative/qualitative divide revisited: A study of published research, doctoral program curricula, and journal editor perceptions. *Journal of Criminal Justice Education*, *19*(3), 383–403.

Cohen, S. (1998). *Against criminology*. Transaction Publishers.
Copes, H., Beaton, B., Ayeni, D., Dabney, D., & Tewksbury, R. (2020). A content analysis of qualitative research published in top criminology and criminal justice journals from 2010 to 2019. *American Journal of Criminal Justice*, *45*(6), 1060–1079.
Copes, H., Brown, A., & Tewksbury, R. (2011). A content analysis of ethnographic research published in top criminology and criminal justice journals from 2000 to 2009. *Journal of Criminal Justice Education*, *22*(3), 341–359.
Copes, H., Tewksbury, R., & Sandberg, S. (2016). Publishing qualitative research in criminology and criminal justice journals. *Journal of Criminal Justice Education*, *27*(1), 121–139.
DiCristina, B. (1997). The quantitative emphasis in criminal justice education. *Journal of Criminal Justice Education*, *8*(2), 181–199.
Fader, J. J. (2018). Keeping classic ethnographic traditions alive in the modern-day academy. In S. K. Rice & M. D. Maltz (eds.), *Doing ethnography in criminology: Discovery through fieldwork* (pp. 129–146). Springer.
Higgins, G. E. (2009). Quantitative versus qualitative methods: Understanding why quantitative methods are predominant in criminology and criminal justice. *Journal of Theoretical and Philosophical Criminology*, *1*, 23–37.
Kleck, G., Tark, J., & Bellows, J. J. (2006). What methods are most frequently used in research in criminology and criminal justice? *Journal of Criminal Justice*, *34*(2), 147–152.
Ross, J. I., Ferrell, J., Mathews, R., & Presdee, M. (2000). IRBs and state crime: A reply to Dr. Niemonen, *Humanity and Society*, *24*(2), 210–212.
Tewksbury, R. (2009). Qualitative versus quantitative methods: Understanding why qualitative methods are superior for criminology and criminal justice. *Journal of Theoretical Criminology, 1*(1), 38–58.
Tewksbury, R., DeMichele, M., & Miller, J. M. (2005). Methodological orientations of articles appearing in criminal justices' top journals: Who publishes what and where. *Journal of Criminal Justice Education*, *16*(2), 265–279.
Woodward, V. H., Webb, M. E., Griffin III, O. H., & Copes, H. (2016). The current state of criminological research in the United States: An examination of research methodologies in criminology and criminal justice journals. *Journal of Criminal Justice Education, 27*(3), 340–361.
Worrall, J. L. (2000). In defense of the "quantoids": More on the reasons for the quantitative emphasis in criminal justice education and research. *Journal of Criminal Justice Education*, *11*(2), 353–360.
Young, J. (2011). *The criminological imagination*. Polity.

Letter 40

DO CRIMINOLOGISTS NEED TO PUBLISH IN CRIMINOLOGY OR CRIMINAL JUSTICE JOURNALS, OR IS IT OKAY TO PUBLISH ARTICLES IN COGNATE FIELDS?

Publishing in discipline-specific journals is the bread and butter of academia in criminology/criminal justice (and most other fields). If you're not publishing in scholarly journals in the discipline, it's tough to be taken seriously as a criminologist.

That said, context matters. First, if none or very little of your scholarship is in criminology/criminal justice journals, that may raise some eyebrows. It's not that publishing outside the field is bad, but many of your colleagues will wonder where your intellectual home is. So, a key question is: What percentage of your work appears in criminology/criminal justice journals and what does not?

Second, not all journals are created equal. There's a pecking order, and if you're trying to establish yourself, it's worth knowing which journals carry the most weight. The goal isn't just to publish but to get your work into the most respected venues that will accept it. That's not to say you should only chase top-tier journals (the rejection rates alone can make that a long road), but being strategic about where you submit is important. And there are numerous venues where you can see a ranking of the prestige of various discipline-specific academic journals.

Third, if you publish in highly ranked generalist journals like the *American Journal of Sociology*, *American Sociological Review*, or *American Political Science Review*, and the work is relevant to criminologists, most people in the field will respect that. But if all your work ends up in print outside criminology/criminal justice, some folks may question whether you (or your scholarship) primarily belong in the discipline, and not in criminology/criminal justice.

DOI: 10.4324/9781003499145-45

This brings up a related point. If the majority of your scholarship is chapters in academic books, even if the books are peer-reviewed, this may cause some of your colleagues or supervisors to question the quality of your work.

The bottom line is that you want a publishing record that reflects your research interests while keeping you anchored in the field. A mix of top-tier criminology/criminal justice journals and well-regarded interdisciplinary outlets is usually a good approach.

Letter 41

MUST CRIMINOLOGISTS WRITE BOOKS, OR IS WRITING PEER-REVIEWED ARTICLES BETTER?[1]

A crucial debate exists in many academic fields regarding the optimal venues for publishing research findings. Some criminologists wonder if it's better to conduct research, write, and publish their work in book format or disseminate the results from their efforts in the context of one or more articles in peer-reviewed journals or chapters in scholarly books.

Unlike other hard or social sciences, however, criminology/criminal justice often sees scholars gravitating toward book publication as a common practice and a way to demonstrate expertise.

Although this is an important issue, it also begs several questions and often involves a series of cost-benefit calculations that need to be made. Nonetheless, numerous academic criminologists are both successful and happy in their careers have never authored, coauthored, edited, or coedited a book yet. There is a time and place in one's scholarly career to publish one's work in each venue. And, apart from turning one's dissertation into a book, there is a stage in one's academic career in which one can or should participate in almost all publishing venues.

Let's take a closer look at what I mean.

Departmental, college, and university expectations about publications for merit pay, tenure, and promotion

When determining what and where to publish, criminologists should primarily consider personal interests, institutional expectations, and career objectives. To begin with, personal interest usually provides the initial spark for research interests. In its earliest stages, it can lead to one or more term papers as a graduate student and perhaps a master's or doctoral dissertation.

DOI: 10.4324/9781003499145-46

This interest, however, does not have to define an academic career. Other things can influence the trajectory of these interests, including boredom, collaboration, grant funding, serendipity, etc.

Next, understanding the unique criteria set by departments, colleges, and universities is crucial, particularly regarding merit pay, promotion and tenure, research grants, and employability elsewhere. Most institutions of higher education in advanced industrialized democracies are relatively transparent about the requirements that instructors and faculty must meet for merit pay, tenure, and promotion. This information is usually available in a faculty handbook on the institution's website. However, considerable variability exists in how different academic entities value various publications. While some institutions equalize all types of publications regardless of prestige, others employ metrics based on field-specific rankings.

For instance, highly ranked journals, like *Criminology* or *Justice Quarterly* or university presses, may hold significant weight in many departments. In contrast, in others, self-published blogs may be considered of equal value (i.e., a publication is a publication). That is why many scholars, recognizing the relative impact that publishing in different venues may have on their careers, scrutinize the rankings of journals (and book publishers) and consult colleagues about their experiences before submitting their work for review to particular targets.

Considering one's career stage is paramount, as expectations can vary widely between early career academics and established scholars. It might be fine to spend your early years as an academic criminologist churning out articles and chapters in scholarly books, but as you advance to full professor, it is generally assumed that you will be editing, co-editing, authoring, or coauthoring one or more books. Additionally, it's essential to acknowledge diverse perspectives on publishing norms, including contrarian views that challenge conventional evaluation criteria.

Not all books are created equal

If writing a book is what you ultimately decide to do, then additional decisions need to be made. First, junior colleagues are often counseled against writing a monograph early in their careers. The rationale behind this advice is that the considerable time and effort required might be better allocated toward producing peer-reviewed articles, enhancing teaching ability, engaging in service commitments, and prioritizing personal well-being through exercise, proper diet, and nurturing relationships with loved ones.

Second, young scholars are sometimes advised to carve their dissertations into publishable articles. In many respects, this approach is easier said than done. Not all dissertations are amenable to being divided into separate parts. Some chapters may be very general (as in mainly a literature review or primarily a methods section) or too esoteric to merit publication.

Third, consider the different types of monographs and the quality of the publisher options. The publishing landscape encompasses a wide spectrum, ranging from textbook and trade publishers to university and scholarly presses.[2] Some university, commercial, and textbook publishers specialize in publishing books on crime, criminology, and criminal justice. And it's worth spending some time looking at their catalog. Otherwise, you're probably wasting both your and the publishing house's time querying or submitting your work to presses that are uninterested in your manuscript's subject matter and approach.

A wide range of types of books exist, including scholarly works, textbooks, and sole-authored, coauthored, and edited volumes. Each format has its advantages and disadvantages. If you're working with a coauthor or coeditor, additional considerations must be addressed, and the earlier, the better (e.g., bylines, theoretical and methodological approach, division of labor, etc.). Thus, it's essential to determine which type of book and publisher best aligns with your objectives and audience.

Fourth, while some criminologists have successfully self-published books, occasionally resorting to crowdfunding platforms like Kickstarter to cover production costs, I advise against this approach. If a book has merit, traditional publishers should bear the upfront expenses. Also, when it comes time for promotion and tenure, self-published books will rarely be reviewed by scholarly journals and hold little sway over most people who review your candidacy.

Fifth, many academics believe that editing a book is inherently simpler than doing research and writing, but this perception is illusory (Ross, 2001; Ross & Shanty, 2009).

Sixth, another frequent strategy is creating a reader. This involves integrating previously published articles and chapters into a cohesive volume. Sometimes this includes writing forewords to each section of the book. However, executing this option, like carving up your dissertation and editing books, is easier said than done and demands at the very least addressing copyright restrictions.

Seventh, specific ideas may not lend themselves well to book-length treatments, particularly those dealing with subjects of a narrow scope. This situation frequently arises when an individual has successfully defended their dissertation and wants to convert it into a book.

Finally, and perhaps most importantly, you must dispel any illusions that your book will achieve runaway bestseller status. I recommend delving into a handful of insightful blog posts written by thought leaders like Seth Godin and Tim Ferriss, who offer sobering advice to people who may hold these beliefs.

Parting words

When all is said and done, sometimes the best thing to do is to stop overthinking and take action. Conduct thorough research, write up your findings, carefully proofread the document you produced, and promptly submit your work to an appropriate publishing target. Too often, we get bogged down deliberating where to publish, delaying the completion of projects we started months (even years) ago. Although challenging, we must break free from this cycle of self-censorship and commit to finishing what we've started. Eventually, you need to take the leap, submit your work, monitor the submission process, and reap the rewards of eventually seeing your efforts come to fruition.

Notes

1 An earlier version of this letter appeared as "Must Academic Criminologists Write Books?" May 12, 2024. https://jeffreyianross.com/must-academic-criminologists-write-books/

2 Beware of "vanity presses." They charge authors a fee to publish their books. It's crucial not only to identify these businesses, but also to research them carefully. Some vanity presses provide professional-quality services, others offer poor editing, low-quality printing, or limited distribution, leaving authors disappointed with the final product.

Suggested reading

Jennings, W. J. Gibson, C. L., Ward, J. T., & Beaver, K. M. (2008). "Which group are you in?" A preliminary investigation of group-based publication trajectories of criminology and criminal justice scholars. *Journal of Criminal Justice Education*, *19*(2), 227–250.

Ross, J. I. (2001). How did I get into this mess anyway: Editing books in criminology and criminal justice. *ACJS Today*, *21*(2), 6–9.

Ross, J., & Shanty, F. (2009). Editing encyclopedias for fun and aggravation. *Publishing Research Quarterly*, *25*(3), 159–169.

Letter 42

SHOULD CRIMINOLOGISTS PARTNER WITH LOCAL CRIMINAL JUSTICE AGENCIES TO CONDUCT RESEARCH?[1]

One of the many questions criminologists, especially those who aspire to become university professors, have is whether they should conduct research in collaboration with local criminal justice organizations or agencies (terms I use interchangeably).

Satisfactorily answering this question is tough, and there is no single, simple answer. Why? There are lots of conflicting messages that criminologists are given, and trying to sort out what makes sense on an individual basis is challenging. For example, depending on a job candidate's background, members of an academic department recruitment committee trying to convince the job candidate that their institution is an attractive employment option may enthusiastically promote the potential for forming research partnerships with local criminal justice agencies, painting a picture of these organizations as welcoming collaborators. However, in practice, these agencies may be far less open to collaboration than is often assumed.

Nevertheless, criminologists working in academic departments should carefully assess the advantages and disadvantages of this path before they invest considerable resources and become totally frustrated with the outcome.

Advantages

There are at least seven benefits when professors from local universities co-produce research with nearby criminal justice agencies (they are ranked here from least to most significant).

To begin with, building a research partnership with a local criminal justice agency may not only facilitate hands-on learning experiences for some of

DOI: 10.4324/9781003499145-47

your more motivated students, but it may also provide data for their master's theses or doctoral dissertations and/or pave the way for future employment.

Working closely with a local criminal justice agency may also provide valuable networking opportunities. This helps build and sustain relationships that may lead to additional future research collaborations or job opportunities.

Moreover, collaborative efforts may result in tangible and practical results, such as reducing crime rates, increasing officer retention, and enhancing community satisfaction. In other words, this type of research might provide an additional practical, relevant, and prosocial dimension to academic work.

Conducting research with a local agency often provides access to valuable data and resources that would otherwise be difficult to obtain.

Collaborative projects with criminal justice organizations may also open doors to additional funding sources (e.g., grants and contracts) that may not be available to criminologists who have not entered partnership arrangements.

Furthermore, the experience gained through partnerships can enrich criminologists' knowledge, skills, and teaching. This enables them to bring real-world examples and insights into their classrooms, benefiting their students.

Finally, and most critically, conducting research with local criminal justice agencies may lead to interesting scholarly publications, which might not have been possible through alternative strategies.

Disadvantages

Partnering with local criminal justice organizations presents significant challenges. There are at least nine prominent drawbacks that criminologists should be aware of.

First, although you might expect any self-respecting criminal justice agency to welcome your expertise and be willing to partner with you, many of these entities may be skeptical of external researchers wanting to observe their activities and review their records and data. Thus, building trust can be difficult, and not all agencies will readily embrace outside assistance. Similarly, agencies may be hesitant to partner due to previous negative experiences with other outside researchers or organizations that have since departed.

Professors or departments within your academic department, university, and beyond may already have research relationships with local criminal justice organizations. These partnerships might lead to collaborative opportunities but are just as likely to lead to real or perceived competition for scarce resources. In other words, your colleagues may feel threatened that you're muscling in on their territory.

Another point to consider is that the objectives and priorities of a university researcher and a criminal justice agency may not always align. For example, the scholar may be interested in improving conditions inside a correctional facility, but the management would rather have you work on employee retention. Similarly, researchers may have to compromise on their autonomy and research agenda, as projects with organizations will likely be guided by the agency's needs and priorities. Also, because of ethical and legal concerns, gaining access to sensitive data may be very hard if not impossible.

Another point to consider is capture. What does this mean? It's complex. To begin with, you don't want to simply be an uncritical arm of the previously mentioned criminal justice–industrial complex. Remaining objective in your relationships with people (and organizations) you've worked with for a long time isn't always straightforward. Your ego might be stroked, and you may become reluctant to report wrongdoing or misplaced priorities within the criminal justice agency and its employees. As a result, you might bury your findings or soften your conclusions. However, if you believe that the agency's policies and practices are making things worse, such as arresting the wrong people or keeping individuals behind bars longer than necessary, then you need to speak up. Of course, there is a time and place for everything, but addressing these issues in an expedient manner and in the proper context is essential.

Most importantly, establishing and maintaining research partnerships usually require long-term commitments. And sometimes, these relationships go bust. For instance, a new police chief/commissioner is hired, someone who worked in a city or a county, on the other side of the country, and that person may want nothing to do with you and/or your university. Or they may have colleagues they worked with in their previous positions with whom they prefer to partner with. They feel most comfortable working with them and decide to continue conducting research together instead of experimenting with new local researchers.

Alternatively, suppose you have a variety of different/diverse scholarly research interests. Or you anticipate taking a job in a location geographically distant from the local criminal justice agency, or are considering moving into university administration (positions where conducting research is much harder to do), then forging a research partnership with a local criminal justice agency might not be wise. In other words, it may be difficult to justify the initial investment in collaboration.

Making peace with your decision

The decision to partner with local criminal justice agencies is complex and should be carefully considered, including conducting a relatively sophisticated cost-benefit calculation. The decision and process should align with your career goals, your department's and the university's organizational culture, the specific agency's needs and receptiveness, and your willingness to make a long-term commitment. While partnerships with local organizations can be rewarding, they also require a nuanced approach to navigate the potential advantages and disadvantages.

Co-producing research with a local criminal justice agency can offer numerous advantages and opportunities for criminologists working at a university. However, this relationship also has its own hurdles and potential disadvantages. Ultimately, the decision to partner and the individual researcher's career goals and interests are personal. Effective communication, clear expectations, and a shared commitment to the partnership's goals can help mitigate some of the challenges and maximize the advantages.

Note

1 An earlier version of this letter appeared as "Should criminologists partner with local criminal justice agencies to conduct research?" September 21, 2023. https://jeffreyianross.com/should-criminologists-partner-with-local-criminal-justice-agencies-to-conduct-research/

Suggested reading

Drawbridge, D. C., Taheri, S. A., & Frost, N. A. (2018). Building and sustaining academic researcher and criminal justice practitioner partnerships: A corrections example. *American Journal of Criminal Justice, 43*(3), 627–640.

Gonzalez-Alcaide, G. Melero-Fuentes, D., Aleixandre-Benavent, R., & Valderrama-Zurian, J-C. (2013). Productivity and collaboration in scientific publications on criminology. *Journal of Criminal Justice Education*, *24*(1), 15–37.

Kennedy, D. M. (2011). *Don't shoot: One man, a street fellowship, and the end of violence in inner-city America*. Bloomsbury.

Lemke, R. (2013). Perceptions on the trend of multi-authored collaboration: Results from a national survey of criminal justice and criminology faculty. *Journal of Criminal Justice Education*, *24*(3), 316–338.

Mazerolle, L. (2014). The power of policing partnerships: Sustaining the gains. *Journal of Experimental Criminology, 10*(1), 341–365.

Rudes, D. S., Viglione, J., Lerch, J., Porter, C., & Taxman, F. S. (2014). Build to sustain: Collaborative partnerships between university researchers and criminal justice practitioners. *Criminal Justice Studies*, *27*(3), 249–263.

Letter 43

DO CRIMINOLOGISTS NEED TO SECURE FUNDING, USUALLY REFERRED TO AS GRANTS OR CONTRACTS?

One of the most persistent questions facing academics, regardless of discipline, is whether they need to secure research grants or contracts as part of their job. Many graduate students, instructional staff, and a significant number of professors don't fully understand how research funding works. They often assume that securing a research grant is "what you do in academia" without a clear grasp of the actual role of grants from and contracts with external organizations. This is especially true in the fields of criminology and criminal justice. Many academics assume that research grants and contracts are fundamental to academic work, but this assumption is often misguided. Instead of viewing grants or contracts as an automatic requirement, scholars should critically evaluate whether external funding is necessary for their research goals.

All things being equal (i.e., unless your chair or dean tells you that it's a precondition for tenure and promotion, or it's written in a formal policies and procedures document) if all you do is produce scholarly research that, for example, critiques criminology/criminal justice theory and the like, then getting a grant or contract is unnecessary. Let me explain some key differences.

Research grants versus contracts

A research grant *enables* you to do research. It gives you summer money, allows you to pay for data collection and analysis, and pays graduate students to do this work. It can also help you buy out your teaching time. A contract is typically to provide a service. One of the most common in the criminology/criminal justice field is the training grant. For instance, a

DOI: 10.4324/9781003499145-48

criminal justice agency wants officers to learn about a new idea or skill that a scholar may have some expertise in. So, they contract with the scholar, department, or university to provide one or more classes, so the officers know about this criminology/criminal justice area.

Functions of research grants

What do you use a research grant for? In general, you use it to pay respondents, remunerate people (usually graduate students), and organizations to collect data (including administering surveys) or do data analysis for you. Grants also pay indirect costs, also known as overhead, to organizational units in your university.[1] More about this in a minute. Understanding these uses can help researchers determine whether seeking grant funding aligns with their actual research needs.

Types and sources of research funding

There are two primary types of funding: Internal and external. Internal funds come from your university. The money can come from your department, dean, provost, president, or a research unit. They are typically small amounts allocated to instructors or professors with the hope that they will then leverage the research produced by this work into securing external funding. External funding comes from government agencies (municipal/county, state, or federal agencies) and foundations. In the United States, the largest funder of criminal justice research is the National Institute of Justice. In the United Kingdom, it's the Home Office; in Australia, it's the Australian Institute of Criminology.

Challenges and emotional toll of grant seeking

Applying for research funding can sometimes feel like begging or that you are acting as a door-to-door salesperson. It can also feel like you are operating a small consulting business but saddled with a lot of bureaucratic university red tape. The rejection rate and process can lead to frustration, discouragement, and depression if grant funding agencies and foundations are not interested in your ideas, or you feel that your proposal is harshly reviewed, and/or the comments that referees offer are irrelevant (in other words, not helpful). However, this is how the system operates; funding agencies support projects and researchers they deem worthwhile, based on their priorities.

The Impact of funding on scholarly influence

Unquestionably, grant funding has assisted some of the most important research in the field of criminology/criminal justice. This includes the numerous police patrol studies sponsored by the National Institute of Justice (e.g., Newark Foot Patrol Experiment (1978–1979), Minneapolis Hot Spots Patrol Study (1990), etc.) and the Islington Crime Survey sponsored by the Home Office in the United Kingdom. But is securing the funding necessary to produce influential research? The simple answer is no.

When colleagues express concerns about funding, I often ask them to consider whether the most cited works in our field required financial support. For added emphasis, I might ask if Karl Marx and Friedrich Engels needed funding to complete *The Communist Manifesto* (*1848*). *Or* if John Kenneth Galbraith needed a grant to produce *The Affluent Society (1958)?* (Then again, these last two examples are often met with blank stares.*)*

Alternatively, here's a helpful exercise: Go to Google Scholar, find the top ten most cited pieces of criminology/criminal justice research, and ask yourself whether those researchers depended on external funding to do the research and writing that led to those publications. In many cases, they produced their most impactful work without it.

Also, be wary about being dependent on grants. In 2025, shortly after Donald Trump was elected president for his second term, along with the assistance of Elon Musk, his administration went on a cost-cutting frenzy. This included instructing all federal agencies to suspend or terminate numerous research grants they were giving to researchers. This had a chilling effect on many instructors, researchers, labs, and universities that depended on this money to conduct empirical research in the field of criminology criminal justice conduct empirical research. The most damaging in the field of criminology/criminal justice was suspending funding to the National Institute of Justice.

Broader applicability beyond criminology

These lessons are not limited to criminology or criminal justice. The same questions about the necessity of grant funding apply across most social sciences and even some humanities fields. Academics in these disciplines should critically assess whether external funding is essential to their work or simply an assumed expectation.

There are plenty of downsides with this model. Some academics spend considerable time writing research proposals, submitting them, and managing grants, including the personnel and centers funded by the grants and contract money they pull in. The demands and pressures needed to run these entities leave many academics feeling stressed and burned out. Add to the hopper the significant percentage of the grant their universities take for overhead. They often wonder if they should start an outside consulting firm and make a clean break from the university. This decision is easier said than done. The middle-range option is to form an LLC, get a Dun & Bradstreet number, and funnel a few grants their way.

Note

1 Indirect costs/overhead provides discretionary funds for chairs, deans, and provost offices, to pay for things like internal grants, faculty travel, and the hiring of students for administrative work.

Suggested reading

Chilton, R. (2001). Viable policy: The impact of federal funding and the need for independent research agendas – The American society of criminology 2000 presidential address. *Criminology*, *39*(1), 1–8.

Ross, J. I. (2000). Grants-R-Us: Inside a federal grant making research agency. *American Behavioral Scientist*, *43*(10), 1704–1723.

Letter 44

IS SECURING RESEARCH FUNDING IN THE CRIMINOLOGY/CRIMINAL JUSTICE FIELD EASIER THAN IN ALLIED DISCIPLINES?

Given the significance of crime and criminal justice as societal issues, one might expect extensive funding for research in these areas. However, the reality is more complex. While some studies, particularly those requiring large datasets, long-term fieldwork, or specialized methodologies, necessitate substantial financial support, many scholars can conduct research and publish without funding. The resource needs largely depend on a study's scope, nature, and methodological demands.

The lion's share of funding will come from government agencies and a few private foundations willing to contribute resources to help researchers do their work.

For investigators seeking grants, the process is typically resource-intensive. Securing funding requires time to identify the appropriate source of money, carefully read the solicitation, and prepare the research proposal, including articulating a well-conceptualized topic and methodology, and being persistent. It also usually needs a unit on a college campus with experience (and expertise) in submitting grant applications to city, state, and federal agencies, not to mention private foundations. The absence of this critical entity may mean your grant application will be quickly dismissed because it is missing the appropriate forms, or the financials don't make sense to the reviewing body.

A strong research proposal must demonstrate deep knowledge of the subject, articulate a clear research plan, align with the funding priorities of the agency/foundation, and convince reviewers that the applicant has the expertise and institutional capacity to complete the project. This often involves strategic coordination with other researchers, their universities, research

DOI: 10.4324/9781003499145-49

centers, or external partners, as well as a thorough understanding of the expectations of the funding agency.

Although this may resemble an academic version of the Catch-22 phenomenon, several factors can enhance the likelihood of securing a grant. A track record of successfully securing grants and managing prior grants with the same agency or foundation is a key advantage, as is a history of publishing research in respectable venues directly related to the proposed study. Institutional support, such as a history of mentoring graduate research assistants, attending grant-writing workshops, and benefiting from on-campus research offices, can also significantly improve a scholar's chances of success.

Despite careful preparation, rejection is common, particularly for early career researchers. Like submitting papers to scholarly journals, applying for grants and contracts is highly competitive, with success rates varying by funding source. While some rejections come with no or limited feedback (especially if you apply to foundations), others provide detailed comments that might help researchers should they choose to revise future application documents. Researchers who incorporate reviewer suggestions, refine their proposals, and persist through multiple submission cycles improve their chances of securing funding over time.

Although the grant process can be lengthy and uncertain, persistence, adaptability, and a strategic approach are key to long-term success in securing research funding.

Letter 45

HOW RELIABLE IS OFFICIAL DATA ON CRIME, CRIMINALS, OR CRIMINAL JUSTICE AGENCIES?

Criminologists routinely work with and attempt to make sense of data. This includes official crime statistics (e.g., Uniform Crime Reports), victimization surveys (e.g., National Crime Victimization Survey), self-report studies, court records, and field notes from ethnographic research.

But not all data is created equal. Some sources are more reliable or informative than others. Just as a chef must be mindful of the quality of ingredients provided by their suppliers, criminologists must critically evaluate the data they use. Data may be incomplete or collected in ways that obscure the behaviors they are meant to represent.

Different forms of data offer distinct advantages and disadvantages. Official statistics provide broad trends but often underreport crimes like sexual assault or domestic violence due to low reporting rates. Victimization surveys help fill these gaps but depend on memory and willingness to disclose sensitive information. Self-report data offer insight into otherwise undetected crimes but may suffer from exaggeration or minimization by respondents. Court records and correctional data are useful for studying sentencing disparities but reflect systemic biases in law enforcement and prosecution. Ethnographic research provides deep contextual understanding but lacks generalizability. Collectively, these data sources offer complementary perspectives but are shaped by institutional practices and social inequalities. Thus, Criminologists must critically assess how data are produced, who is excluded, and what assumptions underlie data collection and interpretation.

What are the implications of this observation? To begin with, it is important to have a healthy skepticism of all data, regardless of who collects it. Even within a small research ecosystem, you, your colleagues, or your

DOI: 10.4324/9781003499145-50

graduate research assistants may make mistakes. This human error is predictable because, as humans, we all make mistakes. We or the people we work with may put data in the wrong column, transpose numbers, etc., and this may be because of eyestrain, distraction or fatigue. And then again, there is also the realization of the dark figure of crime and crime numbers. Just because something is recorded by an official (as in a government) agency does not mean that it represents the big or wider picture.

Letter 46

SHOULD CRIMINOLOGISTS GIVE PREFERENCE TO DATA THAT IS COLLECTED VIA LIVED EXPERIENCE?[1]

As some people opine, seeing is believing, but not only is this an overused, tropish idea, it reflects an overly simplistic opinion of lived experience.

Over the past few decades, criminology and criminal justice have introduced and, in some cases, embraced the concept of lived experience. In this context, the term "lived experience" is typically a proxy for experience gained by incarceration. This concept, however, has expanded not simply to people who are or have been incarcerated, but also to those who are justice-involved or justice-impacted.

The term lived experience is in many respects politically charged, and the current tendency to use the expressions or terms formerly incarcerated or returning citizens, by well-meaning activists and academics, people working in the field of restorative justice, and the perpetual bomb throwers, who somehow magically show up during these discussions, is short-sighted. Worse, there is often an implicit suggestion that the scholarship that has been done to date using the terms related to the label ex-convict (including convict, felon, inmate, or prisoner) is somewhat suspect. Regardless of the misapplication of these terms, here are a few things to consider.

Just because someone has spent time behind bars does not mean they can translate their experiences into something useful for an academic or policy audience. There is also the reverse tendency to elevate (or reify) what they have to say. A considerable amount of confusion surrounds the concepts and utility of lived and practitioner (or field) experience as methods to inform scholarly research.

Part of the reason may be that many people fail to consider how knowledge and expertise are acquired and the relative contributions and limitations of

DOI: 10.4324/9781003499145-51

lived and practitioner experience in informing scholarly research.Knowledge and expertise about a field may be accumulated in various ways.

In general, and in simplest terms, there are two principal methods.

The first approach typically starts with earning a formal education, which includes progressing through different and more challenging stages (e.g., bachelor's, master's, and doctoral degrees). During this training and credentialization process, you conduct research and subject it to peer review. This is a long and sometimes painful process. However, over time, hopefully, this work will provide significant insights to move the scholarly discipline forward.

The second method is derived from lived or practitioner experience. In this case, you work in a particular field, like policing or social work, and over a considerable period, you're exposed to several different situations and challenges, and learn how to effectively deal with them. Alternatively, you're frequently part of the subject population that practitioners focus on or work closely and regularly with. In criminal justice, this role may encompass being a criminal/perpetrator, district attorney, judge, or victim of a crime. And thus, you learn about various subtle dynamics rarely experienced by outsiders.

Why might lived or practitioner experience be helpful for academics?

It can help them understand a variety of subtleties concerning a person, organization, or situation that they may not be aware of and/or have ignored.

It might also assist scholars in understanding selected elements of a discipline, but its value is typically context-specific.

The fact that an academic may have interned at a police department or in a court system at some point in time in their life or career, or they consult for a police department, is not the same as being in the trenches as a practitioner for an extended period.

On the other hand, spending a considerable amount of time as a practitioner, such as a correctional officer, and rising up through the ranks over a significant period may expose that person to many different people and situations. Still, it does not mean they understand the concerns of scholars specializing in a relevant discipline. Likewise, a well-respected gang member may know how to survive on the mean streets, but this does not suggest that they are well-versed in criminological theory.

Thus, it's important to critically analyze the merits of academic research, particularly its ability to represent the lived reality of people, places, and situations. We should also not assume that all lived or practitioner experiences are the same or can equally assist us in understanding our relative academic disciplines.

In short, although practical and lived experience can inform our scholarship, it is not a substitute for rigorous investigation and scholarship.

Note

1 This letter builds upon my blog posts, "What's in a Name? Exconvict, Formerly Incarcerated, or Returning Citizen?" (October 7, 2021), https://jeffreyianross.com/whats-in-a-name-convict-formerly-incarcerated-or-returning-citizen/ and "Although Lived or Practitioner Experience May Be Helpful in Understanding a Field, It's Not an End in and of Itself." December 16, 2021. https://jeffreyianross.com/although-lived-or-practitioner-experience-may-be-helpful-in-understanding-a-field-its-not-an-end-in-and-of-itself/

Service

Letter 47

SHOULD ASPIRING CRIMINOLOGISTS JOIN THE PROMINENT LEARNED SOCIETIES IN THEIR FIELD?[1]

Whether it's the Boy Scouts or Girl Guides, the Sunday church choir, or a pickup basketball game, many individuals enjoy participating in formal and informal groups and organizations.

Being part of an entity can offer numerous direct and indirect benefits, including a sense of affiliation, camaraderie, and personal meaning. Organizations also serve as social hubs where individuals can receive and reciprocate mentorship with others. Groups function as social units where like-minded people can experience a sense of community.

These dynamics are not exclusive to casual settings but occur when individuals become members of professional and learned societies. In most academic disciplines, whether in the hard sciences (e.g., chemistry, physics, etc.) or the soft sciences (e.g., anthropology, political science, sociology, etc.), learned societies play a pivotal role in providing career and existential support.

What sorts of benefits do learned societies provide to their membership?

Learned societies, regardless of the subject matter specialization and the country/region they operate in, typically and regularly:

- communicate with their members (usually through email, social media, newsletters, or a scholarly journal);
- advocate on their behalf;
- distribute information about new developments in the field;

DOI: 10.4324/9781003499145-52

- share job, publication, and grant opportunities;
- hold meetings (also called conferences);
- but most importantly, are places to network.

However, not all learned societies are the same, nor do they equally represent the interests of all members. They vary based not only on the subject matter members specialize in and their relative expertise, but also on their size, management, demographic composition, and geographic concentration/scope (e.g., local, regional, national, international, etc.).

What learned organizations are there for aspiring criminologists?

In general, the learned organizations in the scholarly field of criminology and criminal justice are not that different from those in other related disciplines. Thus, graduate students and untenured assistant professors in criminology and criminal justice should understand the breadth and depth of these learned societies. In other words, it is helpful to understand what they can and cannot do for you.

How does one join and participate in criminology/criminal justice learned societies?

A simple web search will produce many organizations specializing in criminology and criminal justice. Although there are professional organizations for criminal justice practitioners, like the American Correctional Association and the International Association for Chiefs of Police, almost every Western country has its own criminology/criminal justice learned society.

The two principal learned societies in criminology/criminal justice in the United States are the American Society of Criminology (ASC) and the Academy of Criminal Justice Sciences (ACJS). The latter is affiliated with various regional criminology/criminal justice learned societies (e.g., the Western Society of Criminology, Southern Criminal Justice Association, etc.).

Even though you live in the United States and plan to continue your career there, it might be interesting to learn about organizations like the British Society of Criminology, the European Society of Criminology, and the Australian and New Zealand Society of Criminology. However, unless you intend to expand your career in those countries or regions, attend their conferences, or have a strong interest in their specific focus areas, joining these societies may not be essential at this time.

It's important, however, to not only read the communications that the ASC and ACJS produce, but to talk to your instructors, professors and colleagues and ask them what they know about these learned societies, with the ultimate goal of determining which one/s you should join and get involved with. In short, some (or none) may be more appropriate to your unique interests, needs, wants, and desires and at your particular stage in your career.

Ultimately, one of the best ways to determine which group is most relevant to you is to join one or more of these organizations. In many respects, becoming a member of the ASC, ACJS, etc. costs relatively little, especially if you're a graduate student or an untenured assistant professor. Some academic departments, colleges, and universities may even pay this fee for you. Another benefit is that if you have to pay a membership fee to learned organizations, they are typically considered tax deductions in most advanced industrialized countries. It's not a lot of money, but every little bit helps.

The future of your membership

Joining one of the relevant criminology/criminal justice societies is just a beginning. However, over time, you can experiment by attending one or more conferences held by the organization/s. This way, you can observe members up close and determine how comfortable you're with criminologists who are not in you department, and in this type of setting. But more critically, it's not just about joining the ASC, ACJS, etc., and observing what goes on; over time, it will be crucial to become actively involved in the activities that these societies conduct.

Note

1 An earlier version of this letter appeared as "Should aspiring criminologists join the prominent learned societies in their field of study?" December 9, 2023. https://jeffreyianross.com/should-aspiring-criminologists-join-the-prominent-learned-societies-in-their-field-of-study/

Suggested reading

Sorenson, J. R., Widmayer, A. G., & Scarpitti, F. R. (1994). Examining the criminal justice and criminological paradigms: An analysis of ACJS and ASC members. *Journal of Criminal Justice Education, 5*(1), 149–166.

Letter 48

IS ATTENDING CONFERENCES IN THE FIELD OF CRIMINOLOGY/ CRIMINAL JUSTICE HELPFUL?

There is no shortage of annual meetings in criminology and criminal justice. Some conferences will be more engaging and beneficial for your career, while others may feel less rewarding. While some may be intellectually stimulating or enjoyable, others can be tedious. The annual meetings of the American Society of Criminology (ASC) and the Academy of Criminal Justice Sciences (ACJS) can significantly shape your professional journey, but it's worth approaching them with realistic expectations.

Most advice on attending these conferences (e.g., Neuilly & Stohr, 2017) is helpful but often generic and applicable to any social scientific field. Attending the meetings of a learned society aligned with your interests, particularly as a graduate student, can be valuable. While membership isn't required, registration fees apply, though student rates are typically lower than they are for working professionals.

My first ASC meeting was as an undergraduate, where I felt a bit awkward but I wasn't too concerned. Later, as a graduate student, I attended meetings held by the ASC, ACJS, and the American Political Science Association, where I presented papers, each offering different experiences and professional opportunities.

While conferences feature numerous scholars, papers, and sessions, not all will be engaging; some will be boring as hell. But the real value goes beyond the presentations. Attending is about connecting with the field's community, making yourself visible to peers and potential employers, and immersing yourself in the profession.

DOI: 10.4324/9781003499145-53

Making connections and the value of face-to-face networking

One of the most significant advantages of attending conferences is meeting the scholars whose work you've read, debated, and/or cited. Seeing these individuals in person allows you to gain a sense of their personalities and how they interact with colleagues and perhaps graduate students, too. Networking this way can be personally and professionally beneficial, as it's often easier to remember someone you've met face-to-face. Networking can occur after a panel or at one or more receptions held by the learned society, divisions, departments, or a publisher.

Attending annual meetings can be incredibly strategic if you're on the job market. Representatives from departments where you have applied are likely to be present to assess whether you might be a good fit. Academic departments, like families, may be open to fresh perspectives, but they primarily value cohesion and rarely want to disrupt their established dynamics. So, conferences are opportunities to make favorable impressions, even as others also form opinions about you.

Another benefit of attending conferences is that panels on professional development are often held for graduate students and aspiring criminologists trying to climb the promotional ladder. Like everything in life, some are more helpful than others, so be clear about your objectives and choose which ones you want to attend or participate in wisely.

The ASC vs. ACJS: Understanding the differences

The ASC and ACJS organizations have slightly different missions; thus, the annual conferences they hold attract different types of attendees and foster slightly different, unique cultures (Sorensen et al., 1994). Here's a quick breakdown:

American Society of Criminology (ASC): This conference strongly emphasizes research and academic scholarship. The attendees include many university-based criminologists, and the annual meetings are typically held in major urban centers like Atlanta, Chicago, Los Angeles, Philadelphia, San Francisco, and Washington, DC. You'll find a larger pool of research-oriented criminologists here, which may be valuable if you aim for an academic career.

Academy of Criminal Justice Sciences (ACJS): The ACJS attracts academics and practitioners. Many attendees hold positions in criminal justice agencies and have at least a master's-level education. This diversity can be helpful if you're interested in applied work or cross-sector collaborations. The ACJS holds its conference in more locations than the ASC. Frequent cities where the annual meetings are held include Denver, San Antonio, Las Vegas, etc.

Knowing these distinctions can help you determine which annual meeting aligns best with your goals.

Conference culture

Conferences often provide informal opportunities to connect with others, especially in more relaxed settings. In the United States, these interactions often occur in common areas of the conference hotel, including lobbies and bars between or after sessions. In the United Kingdom, the British Society of Criminology (BSC) annual meetings are typically held at universities, with attendees gathering in campus venues such as cafeterias or dining halls. Regardless of the location, these informal moments offer a chance to see a different side of your peers and can make networking feel more natural and accessible.

For those who may find large conferences overwhelming, consider starting small by attending departmental brown-bag sessions. Alternatively, you might try going to one or more criminal justice-related public panels (typically sponsored by local criminal justice organizations) in the cities where you live, work, or attend school. But the utility of networking at these events is often limited in terms of who attends and their direct relevance to what you have chosen to specialize in.

As you move up the ladder of size, numerous regional academic criminal justice organizations sponsor annual meetings. These include the Northeastern Association of Criminal Justice Sciences, the Southern Criminal Justice Association, and the Midwestern Criminal Justice Association. According to Neuilly and Stohr (2017),

> Other than the wonderful career connections one makes at regional meetings, they are places which are more relaxed and friendly in that all of the presentations are in one to five rooms (depending on the size of the regional meeting). Because you tend to see the same people at different panels or functions, you get to know them and make new friends and colleagues in the discipline. (p.44)

You also learn who you want to avoid as collaborators and colleagues.

These scholars add,

> There is less balkanization of ideas and research at regional organizations, which enhances creativity, not to mention appreciation for the work of one's colleagues. This means that people tend to be exposed to research and presenters and would normally not be at a larger meeting. Police scholars will tend to hear presentations on correctional research, and academics specializing in courts and law will become familiar with the predominant theories of crime. (p. 44)

That is why I always recommend to colleagues that if they only attend (and present a paper) at the ASC and never attend the ACJS, they should, at the very least, do it once and vice versa. Likewise, criminologists should attend a professional practitioner meeting once or twice. So, for example, if they are policing scholars, they should try to participate (e.g., present a paper at the annual meeting of the International Chiefs of Police conference, or if they are corrections scholars, then they should attend the annual meeting of the American Correctional Association).

If you regularly go to these events, then you may be able to meet criminal justice practitioners and leaders in a concentrated, more relaxed, and less intimidating setting and help build a valuable professional network.

Financing your attendance

Graduate students may have challenges securing funding (in whole or in part) to attend conferences. Your chances of getting funded increase if you're presenting a paper. Some departments provide financial support, but this is often limited and may come with certain conditions, such as only covering annual meetings co-sponsored by the department or held in the city where the university is based. If departmental funding isn't available, you may need to consider self-funding options and plan accordingly. Either way, it's wise to inquire about funding well in advance of the meeting to avoid last-minute financial surprises.

Conference etiquette and preparing for the experience

Conferences bring out a polished side of academic life. Thus, don't be surprised if it's the first time you see some of your colleagues in suits or professional attire. This formal presentation can be surprising, but it underscores the professional tone of these events. Here are a few tips to make a positive impression and help you make the most of your time.

1. *Plan*: Review the schedule and highlight sessions and social events you don't want to miss.
2. *Be open to conversations*: Use breaks and social events to introduce yourself, ask questions, and learn about others' work.
3. *Act professionally*: Although conferences tend to be relaxed, remember that you're representing yourself and your department.

Neuilly and Stohr (2017) also argue that conferences will help you find your tribe. "One's tribe in this context means those with whom you have things in common; those whose company and conversation you enjoy; those who are most like you" (p. 50). They add,

> being part of a tribe provides protection from the vagaries of academic life. You not only are part of a group like yourself and gain from all of the warmth and comfort that it provides, but it insulates you from colleagues or institutions or a world that is less than supportive. (p. 51)

Another advantage of attending annual meetings is traveling to cities you may not have visited. Keep in mind that they are not always locations that are on your bucket list and that you're approaching these destinations from a tourist's gaze. However, it's important to build in time to see the sights and not just hang out at the hotel bar. There will be criminal justice-related things to do, like visiting local jails or prisons, tours of police facilities, or visits to the medical examiner's office. Sometimes, these are sponsored or organized by the learned societies, and other times, you have to make your arrangements beforehand.

Attending the publisher's booths, display area, or section can also be helpful. This is a good place to get valuable information on the book publishing process and what book titles are trending. Acquisition editors and market reps may explain the process regarding how they select books for review and publishing, how they market them, trends in publishing, etc. These individuals are generally thoughtful, friendly, and hard-working, and getting to know them well can blossom into mutually beneficial long-term relationships.

Final words

Attending conferences is an investment in your career. The sessions can vary in quality, but the potential for learning and networking is high. By attending annual meetings, I often learn about new theories, bodies of research, research methods, researchers, books, and articles I've never heard of. Over time, you'll find that these events help you build connections and navigate the academic community with greater confidence. And remember, whether at the ASC, the ACJS, or other similar gatherings, the people you meet and the impressions you make are often as valuable as the research papers that are presented.

Nonetheless, it's critical to meet many of the people whose work you read face-to-face to see them in action and how they interact with others. Keep in mind, however, that many attendees will be on their best behavior. If you're on the job market and have applied for a position in a particular department, one or more members of that department may be in the audience checking you out, when you deliver a paper. They are trying to determine whether you would be a good fit for their department. Like families, departments value stability and are cautious about changes that might unsettle existing dynamics.

You might notice a different type of person attending the ASC versus the ACJS, including variations in academic positions and their disposition toward scholarship, teaching, service, etc. The ACJS seems to attract more current and former practitioners, many of whom earned only a master's degree. This body holds its annual meeting in a wide variety of locations. On the other hand, the ASC tends to bring together a disproportionate number of criminologists who are researchers.

If attending a professional conference seems intimidating, consider attending brown bags in your department, college, or university. Also, in many big cities like Washington, DC, New York, and Chicago, at least once a week, there is a panel that is open to the public that has criminal justice-related content. It can be helpful to attend one or more of these regularly. It's a great way to connect with local criminal justice agency individuals in your field.

Conferences are an investment in your career. Beyond panels and papers, they offer opportunities to connect with colleagues and build professional networks. Participating in sessions, attending receptions, and taking advantage of informal gatherings can help you find mentors, collaborators, and a sense of your role within the field. Whether pursuing research or applied work, approaching conferences with curiosity and preparation can provide benefits far beyond the sessions themselves.

Suggested reading

Neuilly, M-A., & Stohr, M. K. (2017). The art of conferencing. *Journal of Criminal Justice Education*, *27*(2), 1–18.

Pfeifer, H. L., Alarid, L. F., Sims, B. A., & Palacios, W. R. (2014). Improving the quality of academy of criminal justice sciences annual meetings: Where do we go from here? *Journal of Criminal Justice Education*, 25(1), 259–274.

Reinhard, D., Stafford, M. C., & Payne, T. C. (2021). COVID-19 and academia: Considering the future of academic conferencing. *Journal of Criminal Justice Education*, *32*(2), 171–175.

Sorensen, J. R., Widmayer, A. G., & Scarpitti, F. R. (1994). Examining the criminal justice and criminological paradigms: An analysis of ACJS and ASC members. *Journal of Criminal Justice Education*, *5*(1), 149–166.

Letter 49

SHOULD ASPIRING CRIMINOLOGISTS BECOME ACTIVE AND TAKE ON LEADERSHIP ROLES IN FIELD-SPECIFIC LEARNED SOCIETIES?

One perennial question graduate students and junior colleagues in my field ask me is whether they should run for and assume leadership roles in a learned society. To begin with, this noble aspiration will primarily help if the society is in the field of criminology and criminal justice.

That being said, some people want to be recognized as the leader of an established organization. They like the expected prestige that having this title conveys. They also think that they will be better respected if they hold these positions. However, they often become disillusioned by the ridiculous amount of tedious work required to do, the unwillingness of colleagues to do the menial labor, and the volume and nature of member complaints. In many respects, it's akin to being the chair of a department, the president of a college or university senate, or a shop steward for a labor union. In these situations, You're a lightning rod for real and imagined discontent. It's sometimes hard not to feel as if you're a kindergarten or preschool teacher solving minor disputes among your students.

According to Neuilly and Stohr (2017),

> Doing service for your regional or national academic organization will not get you tenure. If you're a professor on the tenure track, it will not get you promoted at your university to Associate or Full professor. On its face, service will not formally assist you in your career in any way. In fact, there might even be supervisors at your university or agency who discourage you from doing service for "outside" (outside of the university or community) organizations such as ACJS or ASC.(p. 49)

DOI: 10.4324/9781003499145-54

I don't wholly agree with them. Sometimes, when candidates are considered for employment, promotion, and/or tenure to demonstrate status in a profession, the committees want to see that people have gravitated to leadership positions in scholarly societies. Also, in some cases, the ability to do service (consequential types of work) for some departments, colleges, and universities is blocked or tightly controlled. Thus, doing service in your profession becomes the only way you can demonstrate to the hiring or promotion and tenure committee that you have done this kind of work.

All in all, leadership in a learned society is all about being a good citizen to one's discipline. Neuilly and Stohr add,

> If people do not step up and do service for their academic organizations, conferences would not happen, or be well-arranged as 90% of what happens there is made possible through the labor of volunteers. Volunteers collect and organize submitted papers into panels/workshops/roundtables; they run the program committee and all the other standing and ad hoc committees of the organization; they run sections and divisions, they sit on boards, they lead organizations, they do reviews for journals owned by those organizations, and they act as editors.(p. 49)

My recommendation is to begin with assisting the learned association at the division level. Volunteer to work on a division newsletter or chair a special committee for a division of the ASC, ACJS, or one of the regional learned organizations, and then take it from there. Other necessary job functions may involve editing the division newsletter, organizing panels for the division, chairing an awards committee, and serving on special committees or task forces. Over time, you will get to know the players and how they interact, and this may open up both leadership and publishing opportunities (Radatz & Slakoff, 2022). In particular, it might be best to work with the division executive first and get a feel for what is needed or required. If you like this challenge, consider running for a position on the executive of that organization. Depending on circumstances (i.e., you find the work at the division level beneficial), you might want to explore similar opportunities with the larger criminology/criminal justice learned organizations.

Suggested reading

Neuilly, M-A., & Stohr, M. K. (2017). The art of conferencing, *Journal of Criminal Justice Education*, 27(2), 1–18.

Radatz, D. L., & Slakoff, D. C. (2022). A practical guide to the criminology and criminal justice job market for doctoral candidates: Pre-market preparation through offers and negotiations. *Journal of Criminal Justice Education*, *33*(3), 368–387.

Letter 50

IS TALKING WITH THE NEWS MEDIA A GOOD IDEA FOR CRIMINOLOGISTS?

Depending on many factors (including your specialization, college or university, and the number and type of news media outlets where you live), reporters, journalists, and other news media support personnel (like bookers) may ask academic criminologists to provide commentary or analysis on crime and criminal justice-related topics. More specifically, news media organizations might contact criminologists for their insights about:

- recent, past, or unusual crimes;
- crime rates, especially violent crime and homicide; and during significant anniversaries of crimes;
- criminal justice agency plans, actions, and responses;
- police shootings and use-of-force issues and incidents; and,
- the hiring of new criminal justice personnel, in particular leaders of criminal justice agencies.

To begin with, although all manner of news media exist, most of the reporters and journalists who interview criminologists typically work for either print or broadcast organizations. Likewise, there are lots of media formats, including live interviews that are conducted in broadcast studios and other situations where interviews are done over the phone or via email. In the latter context, the reporter may only be interested in extracting a short quote or tiny clip from the entire time they talk with you (the source), something to integrate into a larger news story or news segment.

Meanwhile, there are numerous types of news media organizations and various kinds of reporters (e.g., general assignment, breaking news, and specialists). Big, established news organizations will have highly specialized

DOI: 10.4324/9781003499145-55

beats, including policing, courts, corrections, and juvenile justice. However, in small-town news outfits, the reporter covering the cops may be the same person covering the local church happenings.

Print journalists, as opposed to broadcast reporters (e.g., radio and television), extract one or more quotes from sources to get their opinion, round out the story they are working on, and put some color in the narrative. Broadcasts can either be live or taped segments in order to get a "sound bite."

Over the past two decades, particularly among the prominent national news networks, there appears to be an increase in the number of subject matter experts (e.g., criminologists) coming to the studio for live segments. Sometimes, you may be asked to appear on a panel with one or more other experts, and the host will ask you and the other guests relevant questions. While this is happening, the producer mixes up the visual component with some B roll footage (shots of an incident or similar ones under discussion). Alternatively, the interview may involve you and the host, and the latter will pepper you with predictable but sometimes irrelevant, incendiary, or provocative questions.

There are also various stages in the interview process, including the initial inquiry or invitation, where the reporter or the production assistant may question you to gauge your subject matter expertise, willingness to participate in an interview, and political leanings. For example, organizations like Fox News Network generally do not want to interview (or have them as guests on a show) criminologists who have strong left-leaning opinions.

Sometimes, your university's media relations department manages the interview process. In this case, the reporter contacts this office and asks who at your university would be best to talk to about a particular subject. Then, one or more media specialists at your institution of higher education contact you.

In the case of live broadcasts, occasionally, you're given the questions that the host will ask beforehand, but more likely, you will be put on the spot. Your ability to sound like more than a babbling idiot depends on your ability to think fast on your feet. Just be aware that the host may ask you provocative questions outside of your subject matter expertise, forcing you to take positions outside of your comfort zone.

Disadvantages of doing news media interviews

Regardless of discipline, many professors and instructional staff dislike talking to the news media. There are many well-founded reasons why. To begin with, responding to news media inquiries can be a major inconvenience and interruption. For instance, earlier in my career, I chose to ditch well-laid plans to make progress on a paper and do grading, not to mention childcare contingencies, to be interviewed. Shortly after arriving at the television station, finding a parking space, having makeup applied, being escorted to a studio, and having a mic attached to my suit jacket, I was told that there was breaking news, and my services were no longer needed. Doing a good job may also include prep, and waiting-around time. This time could be better spent doing other, more pressing, and enjoyable things.

Interviews can also be exhausting. One day, I conducted eight interviews in connection with the DC Beltway sniper shootings (October 2002), starting at 8:00 a.m. and ending at 11:00 p.m. I could have said no at any point. However, it was an interesting and exciting situation, and I believed that it was important to provide thoughtful commentary on a necessary and developing local crime story.

Professors and instructors may find news media inquiries needless, inconvenient and time-consuming interruptions. Their public comments may also lead to unwarranted criticism from people who read, listen to, or watch their commentary in the news. Like a consulting gig, many professors think they should be paid for their efforts. After all, someone other than a colleague, student, or journal editor asks you for your expert opinion, but being paid for a news media interview is rare.

Also, although your dean, provost, or university president may like that you're quoted by the news media or appear on the news, if your opinions are highly controversial or you seem foolish, you risk making university personnel cringe every time you appear on the news. Your frequent appearances may also foster jealousy among some of your colleagues.

Many professors and instructors also worry that they will say something inaccurate or silly or that their comments will be taken out of context, and if made public, negatively haunt them. This is more of a problem with live broadcast news organizations, but if the media in question is print (i.e., newspapers, magazines, etc.) or all they want is a clip, then this is less likely to occur. You can always tell a reporter not to include what you just said in the broadcast or article they will write.

Finally, if you comment on a provocative subject, be prepared for pushback and maybe even hate mail or calls. Earlier in my career, I was on Bill O'Reilly (a former controversial host on Fox News Network) and questioned the evidence upon which he claimed that there was an increase in crime in New York City. The producers liked what I did because my comments added a little drama to the segment, and they thrived on this kind of attention. Over the subsequent 24 hours, however, I got lots of emails and phone messages calling me all sorts of names and questioning my expertise. Thus, if you're sensitive to criticism, you might think twice about which news media outlets and formats you're willing to cooperate with and which topics you prefer to act as a subject matter expert.

Advantages of serving as a news media source

There are numerous benefits to acting as a source and being interviewed by the news media. Talking with journalists about significant aspects of crime and criminal justice can be a way to break up the monotony of your day. For me, speaking with the news media has generally been a relatively enjoyable experience.

Talking with the news media is also a way of educating both the reporters and the public about critical issues concerning crime, criminality, and criminal justice. Barak (2007), for example, conceptualizes such engagement as "newsmaking criminology," emphasizing the role of criminologists in shaping public discourse through media commentary and critique. Key principles include challenging misconceptions reporters and the public may have about crime and crime control; making criminological research accessible to the public; influencing policy and public opinion; and critiquing power structures.

Although professors, researchers, and instructional staff interviewed by the news media are generally not paid for their time, occasionally, there may be other benefits. Some years back, a news organization paid for my trip from Washington, DC, to New York, including two nights in a decent hotel and meals. But this sort of arrangement rarely occurs in this day and age of shrinking newsroom budgets, not to mention the rise of Zoom, Teams, and FaceTime interviews.

Another advantage for professors is that talking with the news media is primarily regarded by universities as community service. Thus, keeping track of these opportunities and listing them on your vita and annual report is necessary. News media appearances may also allow you to test some of your ideas with an audience beyond your students and colleagues.

Also, as I've advised, it's critical to periodically get out of your lane, especially if this means trying something new or different. Given the importance of the news media in shaping the public's and politicians' ideas about crime and criminal justice, acting as a credible source for the news media isn't only a way to see how this necessary platform works regarding news gathering and creation. It's an important communication channel to correct things or to set the record straight about one or more of your subject areas. Most importantly, if adequately conveyed by the news media, your expertise in criminology and criminal justice can minimize sensationalism, biases, and oversimplification in the reporting process.

What sorts of questions do crime reporters ask?

Many of the questions that crime reporters routinely pose to criminologists are not requests for specialized expertise so much as invitations for speculation, what we might call *blue-sky thinking*. These include questions like:

- What sorts of evidence are police looking for?
- How substantial is the evidence investigators currently have?
- Is crime going up or down?
- Will the homicide rate rise or fall this year?
- Are certain types of crime likely to increase?
- Will the mayor be hiring a new police chief?
- What do I think about a proposed new criminal law?
- Does the prosecution have enough evidence to convict [insert defendant]?

Any reasonably informed person who follows the news and understands basic logic could offer a semi-intelligent answer to these questions. And often, that's all the reporter is looking for. But I'm a criminologist, not a pundit, and those roles are not the same thing.

Reporters sometimes ask criminologists some of the most inane questions. I often call them the "inside the mind of the serial killer" segments, where the expert is expected to do a lot of speculation. Questions like, "What do you suppose the perpetrator is thinking right now?" makes me want to respond, How the fuck should I know? Then it's those annual commentary-type questions on the crime or homicide rate. In and around Christmas time, especially if it has been a "slow news" week, a reporter will inadvertently reach out to me and many of my colleagues and ask about the increasing or decreasing crime rate over the past year. Alternatively, they may ask a question like, do you think the newly installed Chief of Police is doing a good job? Again, I often feel, why do you think I'm in a position to know this kind of information?

Too often, media questions in this space ask for predictions, unfounded assessments of ongoing investigations, or opinions based on incomplete public information. These kinds of questions conflate expert analysis with informed guessing, flattening the distinction between someone who has studied criminal justice systems for decades and someone offering hot takes based on headlines.

If journalists want to elevate the public conversation, they could start by asking questions that genuinely require disciplinary expertise. For example:

- How does this case compare to broader patterns in policing or prosecution?
- What do we know from past research about the effectiveness of laws like the one being proposed?

- What structural factors might be shaping the current spike in [type of crime]?
- What blind spots tend to appear in media coverage of violent crime?

These questions move us from reactive commentary toward informed analysis, something both more rigorous and ultimately more useful to the public.

How can news media interviews be optimized for a positive experience?

Some criminologists are interviewed more frequently by the news media than others. This happens for various reasons (e.g., they are more inclined to answer their phone when someone they don't recognize calls them). If this is something you aspire to do (i.e., be interviewed by the news media), you must have appropriate subject matter expertise, and it helps if you're articulate and reasonably accessible.

Given the fast-paced nature of most journalism, reporters often operate under tight deadlines. This means you can't unnecessarily postpone responding to news media inquiries and expect continued interest from the media professionals. Timeliness is crucial.

Also, once you agree to be interviewed, journalists and hosts will pose various questions related to the criminology and criminal justice field. Although you may be tempted to answer every question, it's advisable to politely decline when confronted with queries beyond your specific area of expertise. If circumstances permit, recommend another knowledgeable expert. Although news media professionals may offer excuses, such as being on deadline, or make appeals to your ego, it's important to remain within your expertise; "staying in your lane" in this situation is key.

Likewise, sometimes, the questions you're asked appear to be designed to provoke extreme positions. Even if you're experienced in public speaking, it's crucial to handle these types of inquiries with caution. Over time, professors and instructors who work with the news media will gradually be able to identify reporters who are not only well-informed about the subject matter they are asking questions about, but are also reliable and interested in learning about the issues. A helpful strategy involves educating media personnel on the subject they are investigating, as many are open to such discussions. Taking this approach enhances interactions with the media, fostering a more informed and productive dialogue. Ultimately, this process can contribute to better-informed decision-making by the public and politicians regarding crime and criminal justice.

Note

An earlier version of this letter appeared as "Should criminologists speak to the news media?" January 22, 2024. https://jeffreyianross.com/should-criminologists-speak-to-the-news-media/

Suggested reading

Barak, G. (2007). Doing newsmaking criminology from within the academy. *Theoretical Criminology, 11*(2), 191–207.

Currie, E. (2007). Against marginality: Arguments for a public criminology. *Theoretical Criminology, 11*(2), 175–190.

Fox, J. A., & Levin, J. (1993). *How to work with the media* (Survival Skills for Scholars) (1st ed.). Sage Publications.

Kraska, P. R. (2020). Reflections from an accidental public scholar. In K. Henne & R. Shah (Eds.), Routledge handbook of public criminologies (pp. 87–94). Routledge.

Tewksbury, R., Miller, A., & DeMichele, M. T. (2006). From the field: Crime, media, and public opinion: Criminologists' role as source of public information. *Journal of Crime and Justice*, *29*(1), 123–142.

Wood, M., Richards, I., & Iliadis, M. (2022). *Criminologists in the media: A study of newsmaking*. Routledge.

PART V

Parting words of wisdom or criminologist for a career[1]

Note

1 With apologies to Sudhir Venkatesh, whose book *Gang Leader for a Day* inspired part of this title. Readers are encouraged to read Marx (1990, 2002) for alternative viewpoints on success and fulfillment as a criminologist.

DOI: 10.4324/9781003499145-56

Letter 51

CONCLUSION

Reflections on career fulfillment as a criminologist[1]

Few people I've met set out to become academic criminologists, and I am no exception. I was never driven by a deep passion for criminology or criminal justice. Being a criminologist has been much like any other job: a mix of engaging, rewarding, and challenging aspects, tempered by occasional drudgery. I've also crossed swords with all manner of people and institutions I've met, negotiated my way through complex academic systems, and learned to navigate and survive the inevitable bureaucratic hurdles of academia.[2]

Still, working as a criminologist always seemed better than other gigs I've done or could have pursued. I'm also mindful that after doing a job for a respectable period, you and others start to see it as a career. And, after more than three decades, like it or not, being a criminologist has become not just a way to make a living, nor simply a role for me (in the way Erving Goffman conceived this term), but part of my identity. As an aside, I often jokingly tell my students (and others) that if it weren't for crime, I would be out of a job.

Rethinking passion, career identity, and considering multipotentiality

I used to envy people whose work seemed perfectly aligned with their life's calling. Over time, however, I realized that I may have misinterpreted their approach to their job or career. Some may not have been entirely truthful, or were perhaps self-deluded, or maybe I was simply reading too much into their choices. Also, beware of people who claim their work is their passion. Half the time, it's probably bullshit. Sometimes it's true, but often it masks something else like, identity overinvestment, or post hoc rationalization.

DOI: 10.4324/9781003499145-57

In short, I've come to realize that meaningful work doesn't require an all-encompassing passion.

Some years back, I determined that I didn't need a singular calling to find fulfillment, and that realization was liberating. A job or career too closely tied to one's identity can feel perilous; each professional setback feels personal, making each so-called bruise more painful.

And, if you're curious about this distinction, contemporary thought leaders such as Seth Godin and Scott Galloway offer a few helpful insights. Godin suggests that mastery comes before passion, while Galloway is critical of our society's overemphasis on passion as a central motivation for choosing a career. He warns that, in addition to soul-crushing disappointment (not every passionate high school footballer will get a position with a team in the National Football League), it can lead to economic marginalization (being poor). Both Godin and Galloway advocate for pursuing something you're highly skilled in (that doesn't completely bore you) and getting well paid for it, while exploring your interests and passions on the side.

I've also considered the concept of "multipotentiality," which describes someone who thrives by pursuing multiple interests rather than a single passion. Although this idea has appeal, it doesn't quite capture my journey either. Instead, I've come to realize that I operate best when I engage with a variety of topics within criminology and criminal justice, even if none dominate my research agenda.

A mentor's perspective: Frank Cullen on academic agency

Early in my career, my colleague and informal mentor Frank Cullen offered advice that has stayed with me. He wrote:

> We are mostly the architects of our own academic careers… the niches we find ourselves in and the "profits" we make or do not make are largely of our own doing… I worry that too many beginning professors feel abandoned when the ill-defined support they anticipated does not arrive. They expect, moreover, that their scholarly work will be "appreciated," their service "rewarded," and their identities "validated… Faculty members… are not part of the 'caring professions'" but rather are too busy trying to keep their own "franchise" in business.(2002, p. 14)

His emphasis on personal agency resonated deeply with me: Whether I felt appreciated or validated wasn't up to my academic department, college, university, colleagues, or the academy. It was entirely up to me to carve out a meaningful path. This has meant avoiding hyperspecialization (which is typically rewarded in academia) and focusing on multiple strong interests rather than searching for a single passion to define my work and life. In other words, while not every aspect of criminology or criminal justice excites me, enough areas of the field keeps me engaged, productive, and relatively happy.

On criminology as a career or job: Finite vs. infinite games

Academia can often foster tunnel vision. It's easy to let the profession consume your identity, and I've encountered colleagues who come to believe their research, teaching, and service are as consequential as finding a cure for cancer. Despite its societal relevance, much criminological scholarship, teaching, and service rarely makes a measurable dent in issues like high crime rates, correctional officer behavior, or police safety. And if it does, it is done piecemeal and over time.

To counterbalance these shortcomings, I've prioritized activities that help me stay grounded, such as spending time with family, starting or maintaining friendships outside academia, and cultivating hobbies, like learning Washoku (traditional Japanese cooking)[3] and practicing a traditional Japanese martial art. These pursuits provide a break from work and remind me that there's a whole big world outside of criminology/criminal justice and academia.

Some other things to think about. According to the Bureau of Labor Statistics' National Longitudinal Survey of Youth (NLSY79), individuals between 18 and 54 held an average of 12.4 jobs. These were jobs, not necessarily distinct careers, which raises an existential question: Is being a criminologist a job or a career?

Like trying on a new garment, some people enter the field of criminology and work as academic criminologists for a short time. Eventually, they realize that this job or career and environment don't suit their personality, lifestyle, or desired income. It may no longer align with their evolving identity, values, purpose, or personal and professional goals. Many then leave the discipline, transitioning to government or research agencies, think tanks, or sometimes leaving the profession altogether. For these individuals, working as a criminologist often feels more like a temporary role than a long-term career.

This is not unique to the field of criminology. Still, the subjects are applied social sciences (e.g., social work, public health, urban planning, human services, etc.). One possibility is academia's demands, including balancing instruction, research, and service. Another may be discomfort surrounding the tension between theory and practice or disillusionment with the criminal justice system, pushing people to reconsider their place within it. Unlike jobs that promise finite outcomes (like completing a work project or deliverable, achieving a certain number of annual sales of a product or service, or earning a promotion and salary bump), working as a criminologist can feel like you're devoting yourself to a project that is infinite in its scope, asking practitioners to grapple with large-scale societal issues without clear solutions. This makes it a profession with a noble purpose and, at times, an exhausting or frustrating pursuit. Some people thrive in that environment, committing for the long haul, while others exit when the emotional or ideological cost becomes too high. This can include poor salary, toxicity, having to move for jobs, and the necessity of long-term solo work.

This brings us to the broader reflection on careers: Can they be seen as a game and if so whar type? Are they a finite or infinite game? According to game theory, finite games have set rules and a clear endpoint, while infinite games are ongoing, with shifting regulations and no defined conclusion. Viewing criminology through this lens offers insight into why some people consider it a career while others regard it as a transient job. For those who thrive on an ever-evolving challenge and view their professional life as an infinite game, criminology represents a lifelong pursuit of understanding and an important but complex societal issue. For others, it becomes a finite game, a role they take on for a limited period before moving on to something with more explicit boundaries or something that better aligns with their personality, career aspirations, or lifestyle choices.

Ultimately, the transitions people make, whether staying in criminology or moving on, aren't unique to this field but reflect broader lifestyle choices. Where they want to live, who they want to live with, and what kind of work suits them at different stages of life all shape their professional decisions. However, for those who leave academic criminology, perhaps it wasn't just a job or a career; it was a chapter in their ongoing journey to find work that feels personally meaningful and sustainable.

The cost and limits of professional identity

Another point worth mentioning. James Baldwin, the famous African American writer and thinker, once said, "The price one pays for pursuing any profession or calling is an intimate knowledge of its ugly side" (from his essay, "Nobody Knows My Name"). Baldwin's wisdom reflects the compromises or less desirable aspects within any profession. His critique highlights the tension between the pursuit of professional success and the need for personal integrity, especially for writers, artists, and thinkers. This insight has encouraged me to maintain a perspective that balances my role as an academic with other important parts of my life.

Jobs and careers are not everything in life. Maybe now is the time to take to heart the stories you've been told about what people regret when they are on their deathbed. It's necessary to recognize our identities outside academia as partners, parents, children, friends, and community members. Not only might we be responsible for caring for others, but we may also enjoy spending time with them. By nurturing these relationships, I'm reminded that academic achievement does not define my worth, nor should it define yours.

Final thoughts on purpose and fulfillment

If you've committed to a career in academia, regardless of discipline, there are a few practices I've found helpful. First, approach your teaching, research, service, and, more importantly, your relationships with intention. It's easy to go on autopilot and get swept up in the job's constant demands, but being mindful about how you spend your time and energy matters. Second, embrace the cliché of "keeping an open mind," not just for your research, teaching, and service, but in how you think about your career itself. I often find myself questioning my path, and staying open has helped me to grow in numerous ways I didn't anticipate. This mindset of curiosity and adaptability is what keeps me engaged in an intellectually challenging field like criminology and criminal justice.

In the end, although I may not have discovered a singular passion to define my career, I've found enough purpose in my work as a criminologist to feel fulfilled. Perhaps that's the most necessary realization: That satisfaction doesn't have to look like passion; it can be built from strong interests, meaningful relationships that have been built along the way, the varied pursuits, and a deliberate engagement with one's work.

Notes

1 Special thanks to Dakota Ross-Cabrera and Natasha J. Cabrera for comments on this letter.
2 As I reflect on what it means to have a career in criminology, rather than a job, a calling, or something else entirely, it may be helpful to refer to the terms outlined in Appendix A.
3 See Ross, Jeffrey Ian, "How Learning How to Cook Japanese Food Improved My Life," October 20, 2022. https://jeffreyianross.com/how-learning-to-cook-japanese-food-improved-my-life/

Suggested reading

Cohen, S. (1998). *Against criminology*. Transaction Publishers.

Cohen, S. (1998). Intellectual skepticism and political commitment: The case of radical criminology. In P. Walton & J. Young (Eds.), *The new criminology* revisited (pp. 98–129). Macmillan.

Currie, E. (1999). Reflections on crime and criminology at the millennium. Western *Criminology Review*, 2(1). Retrieved February 17, 2025, from http://www.westerncriminology.org/documents/WCR/v02n1/currie/currie.html

Gabbidon, S. L., & Higgins, G. E. (2012). The life of an academic: Examining the correlates of job satisfaction among criminology/criminal justice faculty. *American Journal of Criminal Justice*, *37*, 669–681.

Hil, R. (1999). Facing change: New directions for critical criminology in the early new millennium. *Western Criminology Review*, 3(2). Retrieved February 17, 2025, from https://www.westerncriminology.org/documents/WCR/v03n2/hil/hil.html

Marx, G. T. (1990). Reflections on academic success and failure: Making it, forsaking it and reshaping it. In B. Berger (Ed.), *Authors of their own lives* (pp. 260–284). University of California Press.

Marx, G. T. (2002). Looking for meaning in all the right places: The search for academic satisfaction. In G. Geis & M. Dodge (Eds.), *The lessons of criminology* (pp. 109–135). Anderson Publishing.

Petersilia, J. (1991). Defending the practical value of criminological research. *The Journal of Research in Crime and Delinquency, 30*(4), 497–505.

Quinney, R. (1993). A life of crime: Criminology and public policy as peacemaking. *Journal of Crime and Justice, 16*(2), 3–9.

Robinson, M. B. (2003). An obligation to make a difference in the real world? Thoughts on the proper role of criminologists and critical criminologists in the 21st century. *Western Criminology Review*, 4(3), 226–238.

APPENDIX A

Clarifying terms: From career to work

I think it's helpful to explain some terms that people and organizations, including myself, often use interchangeably and mistakenly. Conflating these words can lead to confusion and frustration about your role, those of others, and/or the objectives in pursuing said roles. Although I offer general definitions, they are a framework to differentiate one concept from another. They are as follows:

Calling: A pursuit that resonates deeply with a person's sense of purpose, often seen as contributing to society and aligning with core values, transcending financial gain or external validation.

Career: A long-term, paid pursuit within a field that often requires specialized skills or expertise and may involve various roles or positions.

Hobby: An interest done regularly, often with dedication, for enjoyment or personal fulfillment. It typically involves learning or developing skills (e.g., painting, gardening, woodworking, collecting stamps, etc.) over time.

Identity: How one perceives oneself, including how job, profession, or work aligns with personal values and self-concept.

Job: Generally, a means of generating income. Jobs are more transactional, with an emphasis on responsibilities over aspirations.

Obsession: An intense, persistent preoccupation with a particular idea, person, or activity, often to an excessive or unhealthy degree.

Occupation: A person's job, profession, or any activity that regularly engages their time and attention.

Passion: Like a calling, this activity usually involves personal enthusiasm or excitement, motivating an individual to invest resources (usually time, money, etc.), whether or not it produces income for the person.

Pastime: Any activity that helps pleasantly pass the time. It's often casual and does not necessarily involve skill-building or regular practice (e.g., watching TV, playing card games, or browsing social media).

Profession: A specialized field usually requiring certification or licensing, governed by standards and/or codes of conduct.

Work: The broadest term here, including any effort directed at achieving a goal or completing tasks (or chores), whether paid or unpaid.

These terms can be rank-ordered based on several criteria, including how much the activity interests you, how enjoyable it is, the level of training it requires, the time it demands in your day, week, or life, the types of benefits it provides (e.g., financial, status, and affiliation), the level of commitment it entails, and the degree of purpose and structure it offers.[1]

That said, not everyone you encounter will use these terms as intended.

Note

1 If appropriately motivated, we could assign a category (e.g., high, medium, low) or ascribe a number to each of these costs and benefits (e.g., 1 out of 10 or 100).

APPENDIX B

Books on the academic profession

Becher, T., & Trowler, P. R. (2001). *Academic Tribes and Territories: Intellectual Enquiry and the Culture of Disciplines (*2nd ed.). Buckingham: Open University Press/SRHE.

Clark, B. R. (1987). *The Academic Life: Small Worlds, Different Worlds.* Princeton, NJ: Carnegie Foundation for the Advancement of Teaching.

Graubard, S. (Ed.) (2001). *The American Academic Profession.* New Brunswick, NJ: Transaction Publishers.

Hall, D. E. (2002). *The Academic Self: An Owner's Manual.* Columbus, OH: Ohio State University Press.

Menges, R. J. (Ed.) (1999). *Faculty in New Jobs: A Guide to Settling in, Becoming Established, and Building Institutional Support.* San Francisco, CA: Jossey Bass.

Mills, C. Wright. (1958). *The Sociological Imagination.* New York, NY: Oxford University Press.

Reisman, D. (1998). *On Higher Education: The Academic Enterprise in an Era of Rising Student Consumerism.* New Brunswick, NJ: Transaction Publishers.

Skelton, N. J. (2013). *The Academic Game: Psychological Strategies for Successfully Completing the Doctorate.* Infinity Publishing.

Tierney, W. G., & Bensimon, E. M. (1996). *Promotion and Tenure: Community and Socialization in Academe.* Albany, NY: State University of New York Press.

Zavattaro, S. M. & Shannon K. Orr (Eds.). (2017). *Reflections on Academic Lives: Identities, Struggles, and Triumphs in Graduate School and Beyond.* New York, NY: Palgrave Macmillan.

ADDITIONAL REFERENCES

Ahlin, E. M. (2020). Broadening the Productivity Lens in Criminology and Criminal Justice: An Exploratory Study of Research Contributions of Master's Degree Program Faculty, 2014-2018. *Journal of Criminal Justice Education, 31*(1): 100-123.

Barranco, R. E., Jennings, W. G., May, D. C., & Wells, M. J. (2016). What Journals are the Most Cited Journals in Criminology and Criminal Justice's 'Big Three' Journals? *Journal of Criminal Justice Education, 17*(1):19–34.

Cohn, E. G. & Farrington, D. P. (2007a). Changes in Scholarly Influence in Major American Criminology and Criminal Justice Journals between 1986 and 2000. *Journal of Criminal Justice Education*, *18*(1): 6–34.

Cohn, E. G. & Farrington, D. P. (2007b). Scholarly Influence in Criminal Justice: Foreword to the Special Issue. *Journal of Criminal Justice Education*, *18*(1):337–339.

Cohn, E. G., Farrington, D. P., & Sorenson, J. R. (2000). Journal publication of Ph.D. graduates from American criminology and criminal justice programs. *Journal of Criminal Justice Education*, *11*(1): 35–49.

Cullen, F. T., & Vose, B. (2014). How to be a successful graduate student. *Journal of Contemporary Criminal Justice*, *30*(4):362-377.

Dooley, B. D. (2016). The emergence of contemporary criminology: An oral history of its development as an independent profession. *Crime, Law and Social Change*, *66*(1): 339–357.

Fahmy, C., & Young, J. T. N. (2015). Invisible Colleagues: The Informal Organization of Knowledge Production in Criminology and Criminal Justice. *Journal of Criminal Justice Education*, *26*(4):423-445.

Farrell, W. & Kotch, L. (2006). Criminal Justice, Sociology and Academia, *The American Sociologist*. *26*(1): 52-61.

Flanagan, T. J. (1990). Criminal Justice Doctoral Programs in the United States and Canada: Findings from a National Survey. *Journal of Criminal Justice Education*, *1*(2):195–213.

Frost, N. A., & Clear, T. R. (2007). Doctoral education in criminology and criminal justice. *Journal of Criminal Justice Education*, *18*(1):35–52.

Greene, J. R., Bynum, T. S., & Webb, V. J. (1984). Patterns of entry, professional identity, and attitudes toward crime-related education: A study of criminal justice and criminology faculty. *Journal of Criminal Justice*, *12*(1): 39–59

Growette Bostaph, L. M., Comer, B. P., & Ropp, J. W. (2021). Factors Influencing Graduate Directors' Referrals to Ph. D. Programs in Criminal Justice and Criminology: A First Look. *Journal of Criminal Justice Education*, *32*(4):391–414.

Hartman, J. L., Bjerregaard, B., & Lord, V. B. (2009). Identifying factors that influence the successful transition of criminal justice transfer students. *Journal of Criminal Justice Education*, *20*(2):173-193.

Hobbs, D. (2015). Criminal Practice: Fieldwork and Improvisation in Difficult Circumstances. In Miller, J. & Palacios, W. R. (Eds.). *Qualitative Research in Criminology*, (pp. 15-34). New York, NY: Routledge Publishers.

Johnson, W. W. (2014b). How to be a successful teacher of professional development. *Journal of Contemporary Criminal Justice, 30*(4):443-454.

Leiber, M. J., Crew, B. K., Wacker, M. E., & Nalla, M. K. (1993). A comparison of transfer and nontransfer students majoring in criminology and criminal justice. *Journal of Criminal Justice Education, 4*(1): 133-151.

Lightfoot, R. C., & Doerner, W. G. (2008). Student success and failure in a graduate Criminology/Criminal Justice program. *American Journal of Criminal Justice*, *33*(1):113–129.

Longmire, D. R. (1982). The New Criminologist's Access to Research Support: Open Arms or Closed Doors? *Rethinking Criminology*. (pp. 19-31). Beverly Hills: Sage.

Lynch, C. G., Young, S. T., & Danner, M. J. (2024). Teaching preparation and professional development coursework in doctoral programs: *The example of criminology and criminal justice. College Teaching, 72*(2): 90–97.

Mears, D. P., Scaggs, S. J., Ladny, R. T., Lindsey, A. M., & Ranson, J. A. (2015). Successful transitions to graduate school: Using orientations to improve student experiences in criminology and criminal justice programs. *Journal of Criminal Justice Education*, *26*(3):283–306.

Murdoch, D. J., O'Doherty, T., & Todd, H. (2020). Preparing and Supporting Graduate Students in Their Role as Teaching Assistants: An Exploration of TA Training in a School of Criminology. *Journal of Criminal Justice Education*, *32*(1):42–59.

Mustaine, E. E. & Tewksbury, R. (2009). Rainmakers: The Most Successful Criminal Justice Scholars and Departments in Research Grant Acquisition. *Journal of Criminal Justice Education*, *20*(1):40–55.

Oliver, W. M. (2016). Celebrating 100 years of Criminal Justice Education, 1916-2016. *Journal of Criminal Justice Education*, *27*(4):455–472.

Pfeifer, H.L., Button, D.M., Summers, M.E., Porter, C.M. & Dmello, J.R. (2023). Academy of Criminal Justice Sciences Doctoral Student Summit: A Model of Professional Development. Journal *of Criminal Justice Education*, *35*(3):1-23.

Pikciunas, K. T., Cooper, J. A., Hanrahan, K. J., & Gavin, S. M. (2016). The future of the academy: who's looking for whom? *Journal of Criminal Justice Education*, *27*(3):362-380.

Radatz, D. L., & Slakoff, D. C. (2022). A practical guide to the criminology and criminal justice job market for doctoral candidates: Pre-market preparation through offers and negotiations. *Journal of Criminal Justice Education*, *33*(3):368-387.

Rodriguez, N. (2023). The Role of Service and Community in Academia: Reflections of a Latina criminologist. *Journal of Criminal Justice Education* *34*(3):306-315.

Savelsberg, J. J., & Flood, S.M. (2004). Criminological knowledge: Period and cohort effects in scholarship. *Criminology*, *42*(4):1009-1042.

Sever, B., Coram, G., & Meltzer, G. (2008). Criminal justice graduate programs at the beginning of the 21st century: a curriculum analysis. *Criminal Justice Review*, *33*(1): 221–49.

Sherman, L. W. (2005). The use and usefulness of criminology, 1751–2005: Enlightened justice and its failures. *The ANNALS of the American Academy of Political and Social Science*, *600*(1): 115–135.

Walker, J. T. (2020). Mentoring Faculty Members, *The Criminologist, 45*(4) (July/August):28.

For Product Safety Concerns and Information please contact our EU representative GPSR@taylorandfrancis.com
Taylor & Francis Verlag GmbH, Kaufingerstraße 24, 80331 München, Germany

www.ingramcontent.com/pod-product-compliance
Lightning Source LLC
LaVergne TN
LVHW010901110826
845149LV00005B/1431

* 9 7 8 1 0 3 2 8 1 2 9 8 4 *